A SHORT HISTORY OF
L A H O R E
AND SOME OF ITS MONUMENTS

NAZIR AHMAD CHAUDHRY

To Mike,

Thank you to you and your family for having us to celebrate together today - so lucky to be a part of the Derek squad and that we have been able to reunite it.

I know you will appreciate this vintage book about the history of Lahore more than anyone; hoping you soon add Urdu to your many languages and can see these sights in person soon.

Daniel 24 Dec 17

SANG–E –MEEL PUBLICATIONS
25-SHAHRAH-E-PAKISTAN (LOWER MALL) LAHORE (PAKISTAN)

954.9143   Nazir Ahmad Chaudhry
            A Short History of Lahore and some
            of its Monuments / Nazir Ahmad
            Chaudhry. - Lahore: Sang-e-Meel
            Publications,   2000.
              148. p. : Photographs.
              Bibliography ; p. 127.
              1. Pakistan-History 2. Lahore-History
            I. Title

2000.
Published by:
Niaz Ahmad
Sang-e-Meel Publications,
Lahore.

ISBN: 969-35-1047-X

Sang-e-Meel Publications
25 Shahrah-e-Pakistan (Lower Mall), P.O. Box 997 Lahore-54000 PAKISTAN
Phones: 7220100-7228143 Fax: 7245101
http://www.sang-e-meel.com e-mail: smp@sang-e-meel.com
Chowk Urdu Bazar Lahore. Pakistan. Phone 7667970
Printed at: Combine Printer Lahore.

Contents

To

The Noble City of Lahore

PREFACE

The ancient city of Lahore is a stuff of dreams in history with its lush green gardens, lofty minarets, mist laden mornings and evenings filled with mystry. This city has a geography of rich architectural heritage and a history, layer upon layer of cheerful people with their lively traditions. As to the landscape it offers rich, complex and baffling tapestry to the visitors. It is not possible in a small book like this to cover everything and so one has to omit a great deal and only present the necessary which is merely a glimpse. Lahore is much more than its monuments, its winding streets and narrow lanes bursting with life weaving between crumbling balconies of the walled city. The booklet is in no way a representation of modern Lahore. The areas outside walled city have just been mentioned as they would need a separate write-up but the rich heritage of Lahore has been covered to a large extent for the benefit of the visitors to Lahore.

As to acknowledgments I am at loss to know from where to begin. Consciously or unconsciously one borrows practically everything from somebody. This is especially so in case of historical accounts and here too there is no exception. A word of gratitude is due to the historians who attempted and left their invaluable accounts and works for our benefit. I am specially grateful to Mr. Farooq Haroon a lover of Lahore for his kindness in helping me as otherwise its completion was becoming difficult. I am indebted to the Librarians of Punjab Public Library, Archaeology Library at Lahore Fort and the Punjab Archives, Civil Secretariat, for their extraordinary courtesy in assisting for this book. Gratitude is likewise due to many of my friends like Ch. Abdul Rashid, Mian Khuda Bakhsh, Ch. Sarwar, Dr. Athar, Iqbal Bosan and Zubair Khan for their valuable advice and help. I am thankful to Ch. Ghulam Hussain and Mr. Noor Ahmad who typed out the script and worked with me in late hours. Mr. Zulfi also laboured a lot. His support, understanding and aesthetic judgement has enriched the presentation. There have been wonderful people who have contributed in countless ways, and most important are my family members, my children, Ali, Farid and Varda whose patience and love in my story telling, encouraged me immeasurably in accomplishing the task.

Lahore 01.01.2000   NAZIR AHMAD CHAUDHRY

INTRODUCTION

Lahore is the Provincial Headquarters of Punjab and cultural capital of Pakistan. It possesses rich reminiscences and interesting historical monuments like any famous city of sub-continent. It has been a seat of many imperial dynasties with its gilded minarets and bulbous domes, crowded streets, busy Bazars and thriving industries which are indicative of its prosperity. It is situated at a point which is historically and politically important and known as camping ground of the early invaders from the north. It is known as classic ground of Alexandar's conquest who left unrelenting foot-prints on the life and culture of local population. Better we call it a cradle of people, religions and civilizations, a crowning position which is established from the archaeological excavations in the region providing proof of its superiority with other cultures in the world around 2000 B.C. Some considering it a bulwark of defence against aggressors and an outpost of the fighting forces. Lahore claims attention of both scholars of history and visitors. It has been a seat of Hindu and Muslim monarchies and focus of struggle on early stages between Islam and Hinduism until Subektegin and Mahmood Ghazanvi established it as a part of Muslim Empire. Lahore and its palaces have many true historical associations. Here in his Royal Palaces did politic Akbar held his cabinet meetings for over 14 years. The Palace has association with loves of Jahangir and Noor Jahan. It is memorable as the birth place of the magnificent Mughal Shah Jahan. It remained capital of the kingdom of Sikhs founded by Ranjit Singh and provincial capital under the British until 1947. It was again capital of Punjab from 1947 to 1955. After 1955 it was capital of West Pakistan with four provinces merging together as one Unit. Lahore reverted back as provincial capital after dismemberment of one Unit in 1970 and since then is continuing as such. Its fate also shared other political vicissitudes when sometimes it was Governor's province, sometimes managed by Martial Law Administrators and when normal political activities resumed it was headed by the Chief Ministers. Since late '80s the process of democratic set up is taking deep roots. The Chief Minister with his Cabinet and a full-fledged legislature occupies Lahore as principal seat of the province. As to city's own development a cursory glance through its history of last 50 years shows no specific measures by the authorities for its planned expansion, growth, development and beautification. No doubt, it was one of the biggest cities of India right from ancient times and many a times its size reduced and expanded with its prosperity but it has been a victim of neglect during the last quite sometime. The influx of migration, shift in population due to industrial growth and scarce resources badly hampered its planned expansion. It is only now that the Government has seriously taken some steps towards its beautification as such. Many of the roads have been widened, repaired, carpetted and parks being restored and added. Efforts to bring in a uniformity of design of commercial buildings and development by agencies is being streamlined to regulate planning of the housing colonies around the city. All this appears good but the results are only to be seen after a couple of years provided the present stream flows in the same strain.

When to visit Lahore? During the summer it is unbearably hot for three or four months and life becomes miserable. But in the cold weather, from November till the middle of March, it is charming. The heart of man could wish for nothing better; but the visitor must be prepared for cold nights. The temperature falls in November and sometimes freezing point is often recorded in December and January. February and March are warmer months than the months that precede them but their minimum is still near 50 ^{0}F. The maximum shade temperatures are between 70 ^{0}F and 80 ^{0}F in December, January and February. They are higher in November and March, but the heat of the day is not unpleasant in these months. The cold season is characterised by fine bright weather. Rain is expected in December, at Christmas, and at intervals during February and March but it interrupts the delights of out-door life for only a day or so at a time. The ordinary clothes which one wears in Europe during the spring are quite appropriate for the Lahore's cold weather, provided that they are supplemented with furs or other protection against the chill which begins with the setting sun and marks the early mornings. At nights the cheery warmth of a fire is essential and modern residences are always provided with spacious fireplaces.

The booklet in hand is certainly not a detailed history of the city, its localities, institutions and other places significant to Lahoris. It is instead a cursory survey of the city's historical fortunes, which it had since its founding and as a camping ground of those coming from the north. Very briefly it starts with its early settlement through the ages and discussed upto 1947 with a brief wind up of the city status after Independence. This, I believe, is required for tourists and visitors to the place. The other aspect covered in the book is some of the important surviving historical monuments which might attract the visitor to see the heritage as it speaks through its monuments. These certainly reflect upon the architecture, art and the then prevailing cultural scene better seen them described. Lahore is not to be judged from the monuments which have survived the wreck of time. The ruthless hands of Afghans, Sikhs and British laboured diligently to deprive it of its architectural enchantments. Many a monuments of surpassing beauty are totally extinct and many deprived of their ornamental details. Much is lost and the left over is not being attended and managed as it should be. With the efforts of the conservationists and those interested in heritage, the present Government has certainly taken positive steps but these require consistency and expert effort both on the part of the public and professionals to save these assets for future; the heritage which this noble city saved for us.

I claim no expertise and the historical account of the city and monuments is an abstraction from various authorities, in brief and concise shape, for the benefit of visitors to Lahore. The brief history comprised in the following pages is an attempt to describe the fortunes of Lahore from its foundation to the present day. It is true that its old buildings do not carry us really far back into the past. But they are excellent specimens of the taste and architecture of the Mughals, during the sixteenth, seventeenth, and eighteenth century and British rule in the 19th and 20th century. We have lost much of the work of Mughal period which would have been as interesting as that which has survived. We have to regret the loss inflicted on Lahore and the tendency which makes each passing generation heedless of its predecessor's works, unconscious that its successors will be equally heedless, and intent only on leaving new records to its own making. More keen is our regret at the irretrievable losses inflicted by sheer vandalism such as that which during Sikh rule and in the early years of the British administration, allowed the destruction of old buildings for the sake of the bricks.

It does'nt appear necessary to narrate and dwell upon any considerable length on the vast changes that took place after British took over from the Sikhs. All the improvements that were effected by way of destruction, pillage and plunder around the city apart, but what is deemed by some to be the valuable contribution of the British rule was the liberty to all classes of people and the authority of State, which ensured protection of its subjects. For example the royal or Badshahi Mosque which had been desecrated by Ranjit Singh, which was used as a store house of powder magazine, was returned to the Muslim community who were allowed its peaceful use for prayers and worship without any restraint. The walled city where bloody feuds were the order of the day during 'Sikha Shahi' presented a Secular Social set up in peace furthering friendly relations. The British allowed religious freedom to a great extent in the city to each community, which had been denied by their predecessors. The Common man appeared busy in attending to his professional work and the city prospered although the havelies, gardens, tombs, domes, outside the walled city were neglected and used for the make-shift arrangements as residences and offices. The period after the year 1947, till late 80s, did not indicate much of a change except that there was lot of movement of population in addition to the people who had migrated from India. This told heavily upon the resources and civic facilities which created problems of ill-planned housing, lack of health and hygiene, poor roads and traffic jams, insufficient accommodation for educational institutions, drinking water and conservation of the left over architectural heritage; which had come down to us. It was in the 80s and early 90s that there appeared an awareness at the instance of public and press, for conservation of city's architectural assets that the Government also realized its responsibility. It is this stage that the city presents a mixed picture of "old and new" with its natural greenery around that one can imagine its grandeur of the past. This was just background and to put one in the picture otherwise Lahore still possesses a rich and magnificent heritage, distinct and individual culture, food, living, values and institutions.

A word about the arrangement of material in the book. The first part is a brief history of the city as it stood through the ages and at the mercy of incoming invaders and hordes; who played with the fortune of the place and its people. Some of them returned after loot and arson but some left their footprints. Some settled and consequently caused birth of a new culture, living and life pattern. Such a change was sometime over all and sometime ephemeral in nature. Thus one will find the fortunes of the city moving with its political history. The second part of the book contains basic and necessary information about some important monuments of the city which are surviving and worth visiting. These also include some of the structures raised during British period which have colonial touch and quite different from the landmarks of the Mughal period. The brief description of each monument includes the known history and something about its architecture.

Fortunately a more enlightened policy by the present regime has removed all fear for the future. The Government now treats its heritage with reverence and has added largely to what has come down to it. Lahore is thus a city which not only attracts those who are interested in memorials of the past but also a centre of official, business, educational and social life second to none in Pakistan. Moreover, the conditions under which it may be visited are as pleasant and comfortable as can be found anywhere in the East.

LAHORE THROUGH THE AGES

BRIEF HISTORY OF LAHORE

Lahore was founded and rose to be a place of importance long before the Muslims came to India. Its connection with the earlier cycle of Puranic legends, the testimony of the Rajputana chronicles and of the annals of Kashmir, and lastly the archaeological discoveries among the ruins in the Punjab, sufficiently prove this. The exact date of its foundation is, as may be supposed, impossible to discover, but one may make an approximate guess about the period of its rise to importance from the following considerations.

In the first place, there is no mention of Lahore, nor of any city with which it may be fairly identified, in the writings of the Greek historians of the expedition of Alexander the Great. Burnes would identify it with Sangala, a city mentioned by Arrian as the stronghold of the Kathoei or Katheri, who occupied the region in which Lahore is situated. But the position of Sangala, three marches from the Ravi-would appear fatal to such a supposition. Yet there is no doubt that Alexander embarked upon the Ravi in the vicinity of Lahore, and must in all probability have passed the site of this city. It may be assumed, therefore, that Lahore, was a place of no importance at the time of the invasion of Alexander.

On the other hand, from the number of coins of the Indo-Bactrian kings discovered, it would appear that Lahore was a place of importance at that period.

It may be inferred, therefore, that Lahore was founded or rose to some importance between the fourth and second centuries B. C.

From the name of the city itself, from Hindu tradition concerning its foundation, from the testimony of the Rajputana annals, and the statements of Muslim Historians writers, it would appear that Lahore was essentially a Rajput city. Its name appears in Muslim writings under the varied forms of Lahor, Lohor, Loher, Lahawar, Lehawar, Luhawar, Lohawar and Laha-nur; in the chronicles of Rajputana it is mentioned under the name of Loh-kot, and in the Deshv Bhag, a compilation from the Puranas, drawn up by order of the erudite Raja Jye Singh Siwae, of Jyepore, it is called Lavpor. The form Laha-nur is probably a corruption, and occurs only, in the writings of Amir Khosro. Lohawar is the oldest and probably the most correct form of the name, as it is the form under which it appears in the writings of Abu Rihan al Beruni, a contemporary and companion of the Emperor Mahmood Ghanzvi, and one who is known to have been well versed in the literature of the Hindus. The termination 'awar' is, no doubt, a corruption of colloquial Sanskrit awara, meaning a fort or enclosure, which is found as a termination in the names of many other Rajput cities as, for instance, Peshawar, Rajawar, commonly called Rajore, and Sonawar, and may still be traced in the Marhatta term awar, a courtyard, and the Hindi and Panjabi 'bar' or 'vara', a cattle-pen or fence. Lohawar, therefore, must signify the "Fort of Loh," and the name will thus correspond in signification with the Loh-kot of the Rajputana chronicles. According to Hindu local tradition, Lahore was founded by Lav or Loh, the son of Rama. According to a Muslim tradition the present city and fortress of Lahore were founded by Malik Ayaz, the friend, counsellor and 1st Muslim Governor of Lahore. His tomb by the Shahalmi Chowk is still greatly revered by the local population and the building has recently been done up with a beautiful small mosque.

These two traditions may be reconciled by supposing that the original Hindu city of Lahore did not occupy exactly its present site, or that the city had been deserted before its final occupation by the Muslims and founded by them de novo. There are reasons which make it probable that the first of these suppositions is correct, and that the older city stood somewhere in the vicinity of the existing locality of Ichra, or about three miles from its present site. In the first place, there is a tradition among the inhabitants of the villages of Ichra and Mozung to this effect; in the next place, the old name of Ichra was Ichra-Lahore, which is still to be found, it is said, upon old documents.

Beyond the fact of its Rajput origin, hardly anything can be recorded of the history of Lahore until the period of the Muslim invasion. In the Raj Tarangini, Lahore is mentioned as a dependency of Lalitaditya, the renowned soverign of Kashmir; in the Deshv Bhaga, it is recorded that, at the end of the (brazen age, Bhim Sen fought Ban Mal, Raja of Lahore, a mighty Prince, with an army of 10,000 horsemen, and after a struggle of three days took him prisoner and made his kingdom tributary; and in the balled poetry of the northern border, "the forest near Lahore, then called "Udinagar," figures as the battle-ground where Rassalu, son of Sal-Vahn, the eponymic hero of Sialkot, fought and slew the monster Rakhas. These stories cannot, indeed, be considered history, but they show the intimate connection of Lahore with the semi-mythic period of Indian history. Numismatic researches tend to show that Lahore formed a portion of the kingdom of Menander and his successors, that it fell successively into the hands of the Scythic dynasties of Azes, Kadphises and Kanerkis, and subsequently under the rule of a Sassanian dynasty of Princes, who reigned between the fourth and seven centuries A. D. It is possible that Kanerkis, whose date is given by Prinsep as about 100 A. D., is the same as the Keneksen of the Mewar chronicle, and the Kanishka of the annals of Kashmir, in which case Lahore must have been the capital of the third Scythian dynasty. However, this may be at the period of the first Muslim invasion, in the latter part of the seventh century of our era we find Lahore in possession of a Chauhan Prince of the family of Ajmer. In A. D. 682, according to Ferishta, the Afghans of Kerman and Peshawar, who had, even at that early period, embraced the religion of the prophet, wrested certain possessions from the Hindu Prince. A war ensued, and in the space of five months seventy battles were fought with varied success, until the Afghans having formed an alliance with the Gakhars compelled the Raja to cede a portion of his territory. The next mention of Lahore is in the Rajputana chronicles, where the Bussas of Lahore, a Rajput tribe, are mentioned as rallying to the defence of Chittors when besieged by Mussalman forces in the beginning of the 9th century.

In A. D. 975, Subektegin, Governor of Khorasan and father of the celebrated Mahmood Ghaznvi , advanced beyond the Indus. He was met by Jaipal, Raja of Lahore, whose dominion is said to have extended from Sirhind to Lamghan, and from Kashmir to Multan. By the advice of a chief of Bhatti tribe the Raja formed an alliance with the Afghans, and with their aid was enabled to withstand the first invasion. On his succession to the throne of Ghazni Subektegin repeated his invasion. A battle eusued in the vicinity of Lamghan. The Raja was defeated, and made overtures for peace. His terms were accepted, and persons sent on the part of Subektegin to receive the balance of the stipulated ransom. On reaching Lahore Jaipal proved faithless, and imprisoned those commissioned to receive the treasure. On receiving intelligence of his perfidy, Subektegin, in the words of Ferishta, "like a foaming torrent hastened towards Hindustan."

Another battle ensued, in which Jaipal was again vanquished and retreated, leaving the territory to the west of the Nilab or Indus in the hands of the invader, and chagrined at his double defeat performed the Hindu sacrifice of Johar (suicide) or devotion, by burning himself to death outside the walls of his captial.

The invader did not retain the conquests he had made;for in A. D. 1008, a confederation, headed by Anangpal, son of Jaipal, again met the advancing army, now commanded by Mahmood Ghaznvi, son and successor of Subektegin, in the vicinity of Peshawar. In the battle which ensued the naphtha balls of the Afghan army, spread dismay among the Hindu soldiery, who fled with a great slaughter. But Lahore was allowed to remain intact for thirteen years longer. Anangpal was succeeded by another Jaipal called Nardjanpal, while Mahmood pushed his conquests into Hindustan. But in A. D. 1022 he suddenly marched down from Kashmir, seized Lahore without opposition. Jaipal II, fled helpless to Ajmer, and the Hindu principality of Lahore was extinguished for ever. A final effort was made by the Hindus in the reign of Maudud, A. D. 1045, to recover their lost sovereignty, but after a fruitless siege of six months they retired without success, "and thus," says Al Beruni, "the sovereignty of India became extinct."

From the above account it will be seen that the princes and people of Lahore played a prominent part in that long-continued struggle between Islam and Hinduism which marks the introduction of the former into India. While

17

Persia was vanquished in three successive battles, and Egypt and the north coast of Africa in less than fifty years, it took upwards of two centuries before Islam had established a footing across the Indus. The strong social action and re-action which have taken place between the two religions in this part of subcontinent may be traced to the fact that the establishment of Islam was thus gradual, and the comparative tolerancy of the earlier Muslim dynasties of India is perhaps referable to the same cause, the result of those long struggles in which Lahore was so conspicuous; for history shows that the steady resistance of a people to the religion and customs of their conquerors will, as was the case with the Moors in Spain, teach even bigots the necessity of toleration.'

During the reigns of the first eight Princes of the, Ghaznvi dynasty, Lahore was governed by Viceroys, but in the reign of Masud III. (A. D. 1102-1118), the seat of Government was removed to Lahore, as the Seljuks having deprived the house of Ghazni of most of its territory in Iran and Turan, the Royal family were compelled to take refuge in their Indian possessions. Lahore appears to have remained the seat of empire until transferred by Muhammad Ghori, the founder of Ghorian dynasty, to Dehli in A. D. 1160. The Ghaznevids, were tolerant race, and to have adopted the "conciliation policy" towards their Hindu subjects; we find them employing troops of Hindu cavalry, and some of them even adopted on their coinage the titles and written character of the conquered race; and their popularity may further be inferred from the continual disturbances which arose at Lahore after their expulsion. Three localities at Lahore are traditionally connected with the Ghaznevid period, and are looked upon as places of great sanctity, the tomb of Malik Ayaz, before alluded to, who is said to have built up the walls of the city and fortress of Lahore; The tomb of Syed Ishaque, in the quadrangle of Wazir Khan's mosque; and lastly, the mausoleum of Hazrat Data Ganj Bakhsh a learned divine of Hajvir in the Province of Ghazni, who most probably came around the invasion of Mahmood Ghaznavi. A writer of many books, he has left a work entitled "Kashf-ul-Mahjub," the "Revelation of the Hidden," but it does not reveal facts connected with the history of his time especially Lahore and Punjab. It is, however, mentioned in other accounts that Lahore was a dependency of Multan.

During the Ghorian and Slave dynasties Lahore was the focus of conspiracies against Government; indeed, it appears throughout the subsequent history of Muslim rule to have been the rendezvous of the Tartar as opposed to the Afghan party. In A. D. 1241 Lahore was taken and plundered by the hordes of Ghangez Khan, and in A. D. 1286 Prince Mohammad, the accomplished son of Sultan-Ghias-ud-Din Balbun, perished in an encounter with the Mughals on the bank of the Ravi, and the poet Amir Khosro was taken prisoner by his side.

During the Khilji and Tughalk dynasties Lahore is not conspicous in the political history of the day; it was once plundered by the Gakhars, and mention is made of Mughal colonists taking up their abode in the vicinity of the city, and the place of their location is still known by the name of Mughalpura.

The year A. D. 1397 is memorable as the date of the invasion of Timur, the "firebrand of the universe." Lahore was taken by a detachment of his forces, and from the fact that Timur did not plunder it in person, it may be inferred that the city was not particularly rich at the time. On his departure Lahore was left in possession of Syed Khizr Khan, an Afghan, whom he appointed Viceroy.

From this period it was alternately in the hands of Gakhars and the ruling dynasty, until in A. D. 1436 it was seized by Behlol Khan Lodhi, one of the Afghan Chiefs, who rose to power on the dissolution of the Tughlak dynasty, and eventually became Emperor. In the reign of his grandson, Sultan Ibrahim, Daulat Khan Lodhi, the Afghan Governor of Lahore, revolted, and invited to his aid the great Chaghatai, Prince Babar, who had long mediated an invasion of Hindustan, which he claimed as the refractor of Timur. In Arabic Mongol is also read as Mughal. Chaghatai was the secibd son of Changez Khan and his successors had established his rule in a Central Asian principality, where later Babar was the ruler thus being of Mongol descent and later married with Iranian and Afghan blood they came to be called Mughal and sometime Chaghatai.

Babar came, saw and conquered. He was met by an Afghan army composed of the supporters of Sultan Ibrahim in the vicinity of Lahore, but it was speedily vanquished. This happened in A. D. 1524. Babar did not remain long at Lahore, but after a halt of but four days marched on for Dehli. He did not, however, get further than Sirhind; on this occasion. Daulat Khan Lodhi, who had invited him to Hindustan, being dissatisfied with his reward of a Jagir, had already commenced to intrigue against him. He therefore returned to Lahore, and having parcelled out the provinces he had conquered among his Bigs, went back to Kabul. The next year Lahore was the hot-bed of intrigues fomented by Daulat Khan. The following year Babar again appeared. An attempt was again made to oppose him at the Ravi near Lahore, but the force melted away before it was attacked, and Babar, without entering Lahore, passed on towards Hindustan. This invasion of A. D. 15 26 was decisive and conclusive

This expedition ended in the decisive victory (at Panipat) over the Afghan Army, the capture of Dehli and the foundation of the Mughal Empire.

It is disappointing that Babar, who always took care to see what was to be seen, and has, in his autobiography, left such graphic descriptions of Kabul, Samarkand and the, environs of Dehli, passes over Lahore in silence. From this one may infer that the city had, at that period, no architectural pretensions.

The reigns of Humayun, Akbar, Jahangir, Shah Jahan and Aurangzeb, the successors of Babar, may be considered the golden period of the history of Lahore. The city again became a place of Royal residence; gardens, tombs,

19

mosques, baradaris sprung up in every direction; the population increased; suburbs grew up; until the city became, in the language of Abu-l-Fazl, "the grand resort of people of all nations," and celebrated for its fine buildings and luxuriant gardens. To this day almost all that is architecturally beautiful at Lahore is referable to this period. In the first place, there grew up with them a new style of architecture, more splendid and elaborate, though less massive than the Pathan, from which it was developed. Bulb-like domes supported on elaborate pendentives; tall minars; lofty semi-domed gateways; ogee arches with feathered edgings, marble lattice windows, and brilliant walls with Kashi work were the characteristics of this style. The use of stone both precious and Semi precious

In the next place it is to the love of the Mughals for the picturesque nature, a pleasing feature in their character, that we owe the construction of some regularly planned gardens with their dense foliage, fountains, and imitative cascades, which have excited the admiration of all travellers to the East. Coming from the well-watered valleys and waving foliage of Ush and Andejan, Babar regarded with disgust the dusty, treeless plains of the Punjab. In his memoris he bitterly complains of the ugliness of the cities of Hindustan. "They have no walled garden," he says, "no artificial water-courses;" and he alludes to the impression of novelty produced by the garden he laid out at Agra. "The men of Hind," he says, "who had never before seen palaces formed in such a plan, or laid out with so much elegance, gave the name of Kabul to the side of the Jamna on which these palaces were built."Lastly, the same appreciation of natural scenery, combined with that solicitude for their dead, which characterizes Tartar races, led to the erection of those numerous garden-enclosed tombs which form a picturesque feature of the environs of every Mughal city. The thought they suggest as they rise, dome after dome from amidst the crowded suburbs, is solemn and impressive.

Prince Kamran, brother of Humayun, when Governor at Lahore, seems to have given the first impulse in this direction. He built a house and a garden at Lahore in the vicinity of Naulakha, extending from thence to the river Ravi. A baradari was also built by Prince Kamran, which is still standing in the middle of the river and reminds one of architectural tastes of the Mughals. This is the oldest specimen of Mughal architecture in Lahore, but has undergone considerable alterations due to its age and repelling the turbulent water bashes.

After Humayun, Sher Shah, appears to have regarded Lahore as a place, (from its Mughal partisanship), politically dangerous, and at one time meditated razing it to the ground, and transferring its inhabitants to Mankot in the Sialkot range; and on his death-bed, lamented his not having done as one of the ommissions of his life. The design was again revived in the reign of his successor, but never carried into effect. After an exile of 14 years, Humayun returned in triumph to Lahore, and was received with every demonstration of joy by the inhabitants.

After his death at Dehli in A. D. 1556, and the accession of Akbar, the peace of Lahore was again disturbed by Hakim, the younger brother of Akbar, who descended from Kabul, of which province he was Governor, and seized Lahore in   A. D. 1563, but was soon expelled; in 1581 he made another attempt, but the siege was raised by the advance of Akbar in person. From A. D. 1584 to A. D. 1598, Akbar made Lahore his head-quarters and undertook from thence the conquest of Kashmir and the operations against the Afghan tribes of the frontier. Lahore remained capital of Indian Empire till 1598.

It was during his residence at Lahore that Akbar would appear to have developed to their greatest extent those principles of religious liberality for which he is so conspicuous. His court was the resort of scholars of every creed, and religious discussions were the order of the day. It is related that the Emperor erected two buildings outside the city for the entertainment of devotees of every kind; one, called Khairpura, for Jews, Gabrs, or fire-worshippers, and Muslims, and another, called Dharmpura, for Hindus. Weekly meetings were held for discussion, in which Bir Bal, Abu-l-Fazl, and other independent thinkers took part. Alchemy, fascination and magic were also practised, according to Historians, the Emperor himself is said to have become an adept in the former art. In the same spirit of eclecticism, Akbar revived the old Persian festival 'Nauroz' in honor of the sun, and appointed Abu-l-Fazll superintendent of fire temples.

It was during this period that some Portuguese Missionaries, at the express request of the king arrived from Goa to the Emperor's Court at Lahore with sanguine hopes of christianizing the country. In their journal they describe Lahore as a "delightful city." On arrival, they continue, they were taken to the Imperial residence, situated " on an island in the river;" being introduced to His Majesty, who is described as "a man about 50 years old, and white like any European, "they presented him with a splendid image of the virgin, and he received it with the greatest admiration". But, not withstanding this good beginning, their hopes of conversion were not realized, and they eventually returned re-infecta to Goa. Akbar's successor, Jahangir, was even more liberal than his father. He allowed some Portuguese Jesuits to establish a mission and build a church at Lahore, and even assigned stipends to the priests. But this, liberality ceased after his death; Shah Jahan more strict Muslim did not encourage the Missionaries; but some traces of the Church still remained when Lahore was visited by the French traveller Thevenot in A. D. 1665.

It was about this period also (A. D. 1584) that Lahore was visited by Messrs. Fitch, Newberry, Leedes and Storey, members of Levant Company. They do not appear to have left any information about Lahore in their travel accounts. The literary circle which followed the Imperial Court appears to have been peculiarly active during its sojourn at Lahore. It was here that the voluminous history of Muslims from the earliest period up to the thousandth year of the Hijri era, compiled by order of the Emperor, was finished and revised; and it was here that the translation of the Mahabharata and the Raj Tarangini into Persian was undertaken. I do not want to inflict upon the reader a lengthy list of the historians, the poets and others who wrote and rhymed and occasionally fought within the walls of Lahore between A. D. 1584 and A. D. 1598.

It is also worthy of remark that Akbar's able minister, Todar Mall, the best Revenue Officer perhaps the Mughal Government ever had, and the ideal of an oriental financier, hailed from Chunian and was then residing inside Bhati Gate in the city of Lahore. He died at Lahore.

During his residence at Lahore Akbar enlarged and repaired the fort. The city was surrounded with a pucca brick wall, a small portion of which still remains around Sheranwala side of the old city. It was repaired in early 1820s by Ranjit Singh. In the fort, up to within a few years of his (Akbar's) departure for Agra, there remained some good specimens of the peculiar style of architecture, but they were nearly all destroyed; the Akbari Mahal, or Chamber of Akbar, had been razed to the ground, and the smaller Takht or Throne-room has been so completely transmogrified by modern additions that it is hardly recognizable as an antique building. The massive gateway, leading from the Eastern side into the fort, was work of Akbar, and its boldness of design contrasts remarkably with the elegant but somewhat finicky architecture of the later buildings.

Other architectural remains of this period are the tomb of Shah Chiragh, used for many purposes, sometimes office and sometime residence and finally now only a tomb; the tomb of Qasim Khan, once the trysting-place of the Lahore wrestlers, and now the residence of the Governor; the tomb of Musa Shah, by the Railway station as one of the few specimens at Lahore of purely Pathan design, and at the same time one of the oldest, if not the earliest, instance at Lahore of the use of coloured tiles as an architectural decoration.

During the reign of Akbar, Lahore, as might have been expected, expanded greatly in size and opulence. Up to this period, according to local tradition, Lahore consisted of a number of detached hamlets; it now grew into an extensive city. The city, par excellence, was that portion surrounded by the wall and covered the same area as the present walled city; but outside the walls were long bazars and thickly populated suburbs which no longer exist now and instead on these ruins modern colonies have sprung up. Abu-l-Fazll, speaks of Lahore as a very great and populous city, famous for its artisans and the excellence of its manufactures. The climate was considered peculiarly salubrious, and it had two special attractions in his eyes from the fact that musk-melons and ice were procurable all the year round in the bazars, with residents equally proud of a typical culture.

The reign of Jahangir commenced with a rebellion, and as usual, Lahore felt the effects of it. Prince Khosro, the eldest son of the Emperor, seized the suburbs of Lahore and laid siege to the citadel. His army was quickly defeated by the Imperial troops, and his adherents dealt with fearful severity.

Seven hundred prisoners were impaled in two rows leading from the gate of Lahore, and the Prince was marched past them in mock dignity on an elephant from Kamran's palace at Naulakha, where he had been temporarily placed, to the fort, where he was kept in close confinement in chains.

The celebrated Sikh Guru Arjun Mal, the fourth successor of Nanak, and compiler of the Adi Granth, rebelled and was imprisoned; and his death, which occurred soon after, is attributed to the rigors of his confinement; though tradition asserts that having obtained permission from guards to bathe in the river Ravi, which flowed by his prison, he miraculously disappeared beneath the stream. Howsoever, this may be, he is regarded by the Sikhs as their first martyr, and his death was one of the causes which changed them from peaceful to a warlike sect, and instilled into their minds a bitter hatred for Muslims. His shrine may be seen near the Mausoleum of Ranjit Singh.

Jahangir was fond of Lahore, though one would have thought that the place would not have had very pleasant associations connected with it. In A. D. 1622, he fixed his Court here, and when he died at Rajauri, in Kashmir, in A. D., 1627, it was his express wish that he should be buried at Lahore. He was buried, accordingly in the garden of Noor Jahan, his devoted wife, and through her exertions the Mausoleum at Shahdra, one of the Chief ornaments of Lahore, was erected in his memory.

Jahangir himself built but little, but Lahore has specimens of his architecture in the greater Khwabagh or Sleeping Palace, the Moti Masjid or Pearl Mosque, for the ladies of the Imperial harem, later used as the Government Treasury (by Sikhs and British), and lastly, the tomb of Anarkali, which, after having served a variety of secular purposes, has ended in becoming the Punjab Archives office after the Church. The first of the these buildings consisted of a large quadrangle with a colonnade on three sides of red stone pillars, intricately carved with bracket capitals, consisting of the figures of peacocks, elephants and griffins. On the centre of the fourth side, which overlooked the Ravi, stood a lofty pavilion, in the Mughal style of architecture, and on either side at the point of contact of the colonnade with the outer wall were two chambers with verandahs of elaborately carved pillars supporting a sloping entablature in the Hindu style. In the quadrangle was a garden, with a 'chabutra' or platform of marble mozaic, and beneath the pavilion and colonnades were underground chambers to serve as a refuge from the heat. Sikh and European disfigurements completely destroyed the effect of this beautiful quadrangle. The pavilion was transmogrified into a mess-room; the colonnades had been walled in and cut up into quarters; but the two chambers remained in tolerable preservation, and are fine specimens of the Hindu-Moslem style of art usually supposed to be peculiar to the time of Akbar. The mosque of Mariam Zamani, by the eastern gateway of the fort, is another specimen of the architecture of this period, and though plain, is interesting as being an example of the transition style between Pathan and Mughal architecture. On the death of Jahangir, Lahore was again the scene of a struggle between rival claimants to the throne, which as usual terminated in the execution of the vanquished. On the one side was Shehryar; the younger son of the later Emperor, supported by the once all-power-full Noor Jahan, whose daughter by her former husband he had married; and on the other, Shah Jahan, supported by his father-in-law, Asif Khan.

Shehryar seized the treasury at Lahore and proclaimed himself Emperor, but he and his adherents were speedily attacked and defeated by the energetic Asif Khan, and the Prince himself, together with the two sons of Jahangir's brother, (Danial), taken prisoners. The Prince and his two cousins were put to death at Lahore, and Shah Jahan and his sons remained the sole direct representatives of the house of Timur.

Noor Jahan survived until A. D. 1646, but her influence extinguished for ever with the death of Shehryar. From that date she lived in seclusion and devoted herself to the memory of her husband. She and a faithful female are buried side by side in the tomb she had constructed during her life-time in friendly proximity to the tomb of her husband and the brother who had caused her downfall.

During the struggle between the sons of Shah Jahan, Lahore was a warm partizan of Dara Shikoh,, the eldest son, and, the rightful heir to the throne. He had fixed his residence at Lahore, and gained great popularity by his engaging manners and generous disposition, and by the interest he took in the welfare of the city, which he improved by the construction of numerous chowks or market-places. He himself collected a history of all the holy men and conventional institution of the place, and had as his spiritual adviser the eminent Lahore saint, Mian Mir. When pursued by his brother Aurangzeb in A. D. 1658, at a time when his cause was almost hopeless, Lahore supplied him with men and money, and when his wife died, during his hurried flight to the Western frontier, Lahore received her last remains. The disasters of his flight to Gujrat, the painful scene near Ahmadabad, as the city closed its gates against him, betrayal and cruel death, are matters beyond the scope of this book, and the reader is referred for an account of them to the graphic pages of Bernier, or the more discriminating narrative of Elphinstone. His name is still held in affectionate remembrance at Lahore.

During the reign of Shah Jahan, Lahore, though no longer the Dar-ul-hukumat or capital, was still a place of importance.It lay on the route of the imperial marches to Kashmir and was the arsenal and rendezvous of the armies despatched to Balkh and the North-Western frontier. It therefore still continued to increase in size and splendour. The palace (fort) was enlarged and beautified under the superintendence of Asif Khan.

On the accession of Aurangzeb in A. D. 1658, Lahore must have fallen off in wealth and populousness from what it was in the days of his predecessors. The absence of the Court and the foundation of Shah-Jahananbad, or New Dehli, had drawn away the bulk of the artificers and trading population to that more favoured locality, and when Bernier passed through it in A. D. 1664 the houses had begun to look dilapidated, and the long, streets of the city to be disfigured with ruins. It was still, however, the capital of the most important Province of the empire, and benefited by the occasional presence of the Emperor during his march to Kashmir at the commencement of the hot season.

The architectural History of Lahore may be said to close with the reign of Aurangzeb and the completion of the Badshahi Masjid.

From the death of Aurangzeb on to the accession of Ranjit Singh the fate of Lahore was singularly unfortunate. As capital of an outlying province, it was naturally the first to suffer from the weakness of the decaying Mughal empire; "ruled over by Governors inadequately supported, it became the 'point d'appui' of Sikh insurrections. The Sikhs, who had been kept under control during his energetic rule, broke out into insurrection under a leader by the name of Banda, and at length seriously threatened Lahore. The Emperor Bahadur Shah, the son and successor of Aurangzeb, marched to Lahore with a view of crushing the rebellion, but died before he could achieve any decisive success over them. His death was followed by the usual struggle among the sons; Azim-usshan, a younger, but more popular, son, edeavoured to seize the throne and oust his elder brother Jehandar. A conflict ensued between the brothers and their respective partizans outside the city walls; Azim-usshan was driven from the field, and fled precipitately to the Ravi; which he endeavoured to cross upon an elephant. But the river, being swollen, swept him away, elephant and all.

The struggles between Jehandar and Farrukh Sieyer for the imperial throne and the dissensions and intrigues in the court of the latter encouraged the Sikhs to further excesses; they defeated the Governor of Lahore, and it became necessary for Farrukh Sieyer to take some measures for their repression; he appointed Abul-Samad Khan, a Turani nobleman and an officer of known vigor, to the Viceroyship of Lahore; he obtained a brilliant success over the rebels, and took Banda himself prisoner and despatched him to Dehli. Abul Samad was succeeded in the Viceroyship by his son, Zikariya Khan, under the title of Khan Bahadur, and for twenty-one years the Punjab was peaceful; the weakness of the court of Dehli turned the Viceroy into a satrap, who, safe for a time in his fountain-lulled palace at Begampura, viewed with complacency the failing powers of the sick man and the rise of the Marhattas.

In November A. D. 1738 the citizens of Lahore heard with dismay of the approach of a new enemy from the West led by the Turkomanni warrior Nadir Kuli Khan, who, from the vale of Azerbijan. On the 18ᵗʰ November A. D. 1738 he crossed the Indus, "passed rapidly, without boat or raft, the Jhelam and Chenab, rivers"-writes his Secretary, Mirza Mehdi,-"furious as the ocean or as arm of a destructive sea," and pushed on for Lahore. A faint show of resistance was made at Wazirabad, and again in the vicinity of Lahore, but to no purpose; and at length the invading army encamped in the gardens of Shalamar.

Zikriya Khan, the Viceroy, had no particular affection for the court of Dehli, and was soon convinced that discretion is the better part of valour. He brought twenty Lacs of rupees and a vast array of elephants and presented them before the throne of the invader, and the result was that Zikariya was confirmed in his Governorship, and Lahore was this time unpillaged.

On the 29ᵗʰ December the troops of Nadir Shah quitted Lahore enroute for Dehli. The prostration of the Mughal empire by the ensuing victory of Karnal and sack of Dehli gave fresh courage to the Sikhs, who had been restrained during the vigorous rule of Abd-ul-Samad and Zikariya Khan; but the latter was now dead, and his son and successor, Yahya Khan, was less fortunate. A marauding band of Sikhs had collected at Eminabad, a locality fraught with sacred recollections to their minds; here is the shrine of Rori Sahib marking the spot where their Guru Nanak, in performance of a vow of penance, knelt down and prayed upon the hard ground. Troops were sent by Yahya Khan to disperse them, but the Sikhs, inspired by the religio loci, fell upon the detachment with fury and overpowered it. The news of this disaster exasperated the Viceroy, who dispatched another overwhelming force under the command of Laghpat Rae, which succeeded in defeating the insurgents.

Two years from this event a more powerful enemy appeared before the walls of Lahore in the person of Ahmad Shah, the successor of Nadir Shah, who had no sooner established himself on the throne than he marched an army into India; the Viceroyship at Lahore was then a bone of contention between the two sons of Zikariya Khan, Yahya and Shah Nawaz Khan, while the Court of Dehli looked on, too weak or too inactive to interfere. To aid his cause, Shah Nawaz encouraged the advance of Ahmad, recollecting that his father had not fared badly at the hands of the Western invader.

So Ahmad Shah advanced; but his army was small, and Shah Nawaz Khan, having prevailed over his brother, thought better of his treachery. He met the invading forces, was disastrously defeated under the walls of the city, and Ahmad Shah took possession of Lahore.

From this time until the establishment of Ranjit Singh's rule, Lahore was subject to periodical invasions, pillage and depopulation, and was thus reduced from a mighty city to little more than a walled township set in a circle of ruinous waste. Quarter after quarter became gradually deserted. The wealthy residents of "Guzar Langar Khan" relinquished their "country seats," and retired for safety within the city wall; the merchants fled in numbers to Amritsar; the artificers were dispersed,-some following the invading armies on their return march to Kabul, others to Hindustan. At length the inhabited portion of the city was confined to the area surrounded by the city wall.

The first invasion of Ahmad Shah, having passed Lahore, met with a check in Sirhind, and the conqueror returned the way he came; Mir Mannu, son of the Dehli Wazir, who had distinguished himself in the battle, was appointed Governor of Lahore. At the close of A. D. 1748 Ahmad Shah again crossed the Indus, but the invasion was warded off partly by the bold front assumed by Mir Mannu at the banks of the Chenab and partly by diplomacy. The following year it was renewed with better success. The invader marched, without opposition, to Lahore, and halted a short distance from the suburb of Shahdarah, where Mir Mannu had entrenched himself. He crossed the river, however, at a ford higher up, and proceeded to invest Lahore,-his own camp being fixed in the vicinity of the Shalamar gardens. For four months Mir Mannu made a good defence. At length, however, as provision and forage began to fall short, he imprudently risked a general action. On the morning of the 12th April 1752 he marched out of his entrenchment and took up a position near the village of Mahmood Buti; a battle ensued which was sustained for some hours with doubtful success on both sides, but at length the tide was turned by a charge of the Durrani horse, and Mir Mannu retired into the citadel. The next morning, however, finding further resistance hopeless, he repaired to the tent of the conqueror to make his submission, when the following dialogue is said to have taken place:-"How is it," said Ahmad Shah, "that you have not, long ere this, come to do homage to your lord and master?" "Because," replied Mir Mannu, "I had another master to serve." "And why," rejoined the Shah sarcastically, "did not your master protect you in this hour of need?" "Because," replied the other proudly, "he knew that Mir Mannu would take care of himself." "And supposing," continued the Shah, "you had been victorious?" "I should have put you in an iron cage and sent you prisoner to Dehli," was the reply. "And now that I am victor, what do you expect at my hands?" "If you are a tradesman," said Mir Mannu, "sell me; if an executioner, put me to death; but if you are a prince, be generous." The conqueror, struck with admiration at the dauntless bearing of his youthful adversary, called him the Rustam of India, decorated him with a jewelled sword, and confirmed him in the post of Viceroy of the Punjab.

But Mir Mannu did not long live to enjoy his newly-acquired title; he died soon afterwards, leaving an infant son and a widow. The latter succeeded as guardian; for a time she vainly endeavoured to keep friends with both Kabul and Dehli; at length, however, her duplicity was discovered, and the Dehli Wazir summarily put an end to her intrigues by having her seized in her own house and carried off a prisoner. This ungallant act afforded the Durrani a pretext for a fourth invasion. Lahore was occupied without opposition and placed under the conqueror's son, Prince Timur; but an act of intolerance on his part in defiling the sacred tank at Amritsar roused the fury of the Sikhs, now a rapidly-rising sect. Sikh horsemen swarmed round the city walls and assumed so threatening an aspect that Prince Timur thought it prudent to retire, and Lahore for the first time fell into the hands of the Sikhs.

Their leader, Jassa Singh, a carpenter, at once assumed the prerogatives of sovereignty, and struck a coin bearing the inscription "Coined by the grace of the Khalsa." Their occupation this time was short-lived (1756-58) and they were expelled by a new enemy in the shape of the Marhattas, under a chief named Ragoba, whom Adina Beg Khan, the deputy of Mir Mannu, had invited to his assistance.

With their help he was installed on the viceregal throne, but he enjoyed his success for a few months. He died leaving a name still held in some respect as part of the last Mughal Government of Lahore.

The success of the Marhattas led to a fifth invasion from Ahmad Shah, which resulted in their disastrous over-throw at Panipat in A. D. 1761. One Buland Khan was made chief of Lahore; but the Government machinery was powerless, and the Sikhs again assumed a formidable appearance, and besieged his successor, Obeid Khan, in the fort of Lahore. A sixth descent of the Duranis scattered the Sikh forces and inflicted on them a terrible slaughter near Ludhianah. He returned via Lahore and left one Kabuli Mal as Governor, and the country ravaged by Sikh horsemen. The success of the Sikhs in Sirhind led Ahmad Shah to undertake his seventh invasion; but he retired somewhat precipitately without having effected his object. Kabuli Mal was ejected, and the Sikhs again became masters of Lahore. In A. D. 1767 Ahmad Shah made his eighth and last invasion.

During thirty years following the final departure of Ahmad Shah the Sikhs were pretty much left to themselves, and increased in wealth and numbers. They gradually divided themselves into independent misls or bands under the command of hereditary chieftains with a common place of meeting at Amritsar.

Lahore meanwhile was portioned out amongst a triumvirate of Sikh chieftains named respectively Gujar Singh, Lehna Singh and Sobha Singh, who are spoken of to this day as the "three hakims". The former had his stronghold in a brick fort between Shalamar and Lahore, which still bears his name; Lehna Singh in the citadel, and Sobha Singh in the garden of Zebinda Begum, which he truned into a fort known of the name of Nawankot.

At length in A. D. 1797 the spell was again broken. Shah Zaman, the successor of Timur on the throne of Kabul, but known in aftertimes as the blind exile of Ludhianah, and the brother of the unfortunate Shah Shujah, made a new attempt to establish a Durani empire from Kabul to the Ganges. His advance created the liveliest sensation not only in the Punjab, but even in the Council Chamber at Calcutta, Governor-Generals wrote long minutes, augmented the native army and laid the foundation of that chronic state of apprehension which ended only in the expedition to Afghanistan.

In the beginning of the cold season Shah Zaman appeared before Lahore, and the tall sheep-skin cap of the then youthful warrior recollected as he rode upon a prancing steed on the plain fronting the citadel. But his expedition was cut short by bad tidings from home, and he returned after exacting a subsidy of 30 Lacs from the few wealthy merchants who still remained.

The next year it was renewed with no better success; but it is interesting as being the first occasion on which Ranjit Singh, son of Maha Singh, chief of the Sukherchakiya Misl, came prominently into notice and made the first step towards obtaining the sovereignty of the Punjab by securing from the retiring Durani emperor a formal grant of the chiefship of Lahore. The history of Lahore is henceforth contained in the history of its ruler, Maharaja Ranjit Singh, the events of whose life are detailed by many writers. The brief resume of events may be given for the information and interest of reader.

In A. D. 1799 Ranjit Singh became master of Lahore, which was then in possession of Sirdar Chait Singh, the son of the "Triumvir" Lehna Singh, after a short struggle in which Ranjit Singh was aided by the treachery of the leading men.

In A. D. 1801 he assumed the title of 'Sirkar', established a mint, and commenced his career as a sovereign. But the Lahore of which Ranjit Singh was now sovereign was a very different place from the Lahore of the Mughal period. From a mighty city it had sunk to the position of a mere township, and even within its dilapidated walls it was but sparsely inhabited; outside was ruin and devastation. The only signs of life were two Sikh forts, built to overawe the country round about, and a few scattered hamlets,-one peopled by the descendants of a hardy clan of Balochs who had settled at Lahore in happier times, and another by a few peasants who clung to the site of the old Hindu city.

29

Perhaps the best idea of the contrast between Lahore of the Mughal Emperors and Lahore of the commencement of this century will be afforded by placing in juxta-position the account of the city as given by Abu-l-Fazll in the reign of Akbar and that given by an European Officer who visited it in A. D. 1809. "Lahore," says Abu-l-Fazll, "is a very large and populous city. The fort and palace are of brick and lime, and when this city was for some time the seat of Government many other capital buildings were erected and gardens laid out in taste and elegance; it became the grand resort of people of all nations, and their manufactures were brought to the highest pitch of perfection." Through His Majesty's (Akbar's) encouragement "gardeners were brought from Iran and Turan, who cultivated the vine and various kinds of melons. The manufactures of silk and woollen carpets were introduced, together with that of brocades;" in short, "here could be obtained the choicest productions of Iran, Turan and Hindustan."

Extract from the Diary of an Officer who visited Lahore in A. D. 1809:- "29th May. I visited the ruins of Lahore, which afforded a melancholy picture of fallen splendour. Here the lofty dwellings and masjids which not fifty years ago raised their tops to the skies, and were the pride of a busy and active population, are now crumbling into dust, and in less than half a century more will be levelled with the ground. In going over these ruins I saw not a human being; all was silence, solitude, and gloom. This city in the days of its glory must have been most splendid."

In A. D. 1802 Ranjit Singh obtained the celebrated gun Zamzamah, a huge piece which Ahmad Shah had used in the battle of Panipat, but had left behind. The gun had hitherto been in possession of the most powerful of the misls, the Bhangis of Amritsar, and came to be regarded as the talisman of Sikh Empire. Hence its capture by Ranjit Singh added greatly to his prestige. From this period the tide of success flowed on apace; Jhang, Kasur, Pathankot, Sialkot, Gujrat felt the power of his arms, and the chiefs of Multan, Jalandhar and Kassauli were glad to ward off an attack by timely submission and acknowledgment of Ranjit Singh as lord paramount.

In A. D. 1812 he became possessed of the person of Shah Shujah and of the Koh-i-Noor, effectually opposed the hitherto irresistible progress of Afghan invaders, and re-occupied the fort of Attock.

In A. D. 1814 he suffered his first reverse in an attempt to conquer Kashmir, but he so far succeeded as to obtain from the Governor a formal recognition of the paramount authority of the Lahore Darbar.

In A. D. 1818 Multan was besieged and taken and the province annexed to the empire of the Maharaja. In 1819 Kashmir was at length conquered. This was followed in 1823 by the capture of Peshawar.

"Ranjit Singh died in A. D. 1839, lord of the Punjab from the Sulaimanni range to the Sutlej and from Kashmir to beyond Multan, an empire little less in extent then that of Jaipal, having a regular army and three hundred pieces of artillery-in fact his rule may be considered an improved edition of the old Rajput dynasty. This empire he raised by his own personal character, working upon a vigorous social confederation, and, as other empires which have been similarly constructed, it was destined to perish mole sua."

The successors of Ranjit Singh threw themselves alternately into the hands of the one party or the other as it suited their interests or caprice, and it thereupon became the object of the party out of favour to put their rivals "out of the way." The first act in the drama was the murder of Chait Singh, a minion, of the imbecile Kharak Singh, Ranjit Singh's successor. This was done in pursuance of a concerted design between Nao Nihal Singh, the heir-apparent, and the Jammu party, but no sooner had the object been attained than Nao Nihal turned against his friends.

Kharak Singh died in 1840; Nao Nihal Singh, who, there is reason to believe, had hastened his father's death by poison, was the same day killed by the fall of a portion of an archway as he was proceeding on foot from witnessing the cremation of his father's remains. The ashes of the father and son rest side by side beneath two small domes to the left of the mausoleum of Ranjit Singh.

The death of Nao Nihal Singh was followed by a struggle between the mother of the deceased prince in concert with the Sindhinwalia party and Sher Singh, a disowned son of Ranjit Singh, aided by Dhian Singh, a favourite of Ranjit Singh. The soi-disant queen-regent, aided, strange to say, by Gulab Singh, the brother of Dhian Singh, held the fort, and Sher Singh had to besiege them. The siege lasted four days, from the 14th to the 18th January 1841. The main attacks of the besiegers were made in the Hazuri Bagh, where Sher Singh took up his position in the then un-finished marble pavilion in front of the massive gateway.

Twelve cannons were directed against the fort walls, and 'zemburahs' or light guns used in the mountain warfare of Kashmir were mounted on the tops of the minarets of the great mosque of Aurangzeb, which overlook the fort. The bombardment resulted in the submission of the queen and her party and the coronation of Sher Singh.

Sher Singh, in his turn, fell a victim to a coalition between the Sindhianwalias and the Dogra chiefs. On the 15th September 1843 he was assassinated by Ajit Singh, the Sindhianwalia chief, Shah Balawal near Lahore.

Having succeeded in their attempt, the Sindhianwalias forthwith turned their hands against their late ally, Raja Dhian Singh, who was shot down and cut to pieces, within an hour of the death of Sher Singh, at the summit of the ascent into the fort from the Hazuri Bagh.

This led to a second siege of Lahore by Hira Singh, son of Dhian Singh, aided by the Khalsa army, animated by the prospect of high pay and plunder. The wall was breached; Ajit Singh, the assassin, sprung over the north-east angle of the fort, and was cut to pieces in the place where he fell; Lehna Singh, already wounded, fell into the hands of the soldiery, and was shot and hacked to death.

For a little more than a year Hira·Singh was virtual ruler in the name of Dulip Singh, the son of the Rani Chandan, a queen of Ranjit Singh; he fell owing to a personal quarrel with the Rani and unpopularity with the fickle Khalsa army. He fled with his adviser, Pandit Jallah, pursued by Jowahir Singh, the Rani's brother, and troops of Khalsa horse; from Shahdra a close pursuit was kept up for some twelve miles, until the unhappy Pandit fell from his horse from exhaustion and was cut to pieces. Hira Singh continued his flight, and headed his pursuers, but, imprudently stopping at a village to get a draught of water was surrounded and slain after a desperate resistance. Jowahir Singh, in his turn, was deliberately shot on parade. Lal Singh, the paramour of Rani Chandan, then became nominally Wazir, but the Government was really the will of the army at Lahore. Irritation at the defensive preparations made by the English Government, restlessness and desire for plunder led to the invasion of British territories on the 11th December 1845, the battles of Moodkee, Ferozeshah, and Sobraon lost, this led to the occupation of Lahore; and then at length-in the words of a local ballad-"sorrow was silenced, and the Sikh empire became a story of the past." A British Resident was posted a Lahore with Army for protection of Lahore Durbar in 1846. Their stay was extended and then followed the first Sikh war and disaster of Multan which led to surrender of Governor Mul Raj. The British had still to fight another battle at Chillianwala (Gujrat) whereafter the Sikhs finally extinguished and Punjab was annexed in March 1849. The transfer of sovereignty took place at Shish Mahal, Lahore fort. The infant Maharaja Dulip Singh was deposed and British occupied the country as victors.

LAHORE DURING BRITISH RULE AND AFTER

The British emerged in complete control of sub-continent in 1849 after they had occupied Punjab and their borders extended to Afghanistan including Kashmir and northern areas touching Central Asia. They planned exploitation of natural resources of Punjab by improving its system of Irrigation, Agriculture and mineral wealth, and were politically accomplishing much more secret mission of containing Russia and securing their borders. While the old Mughal king Bahadur Shah Zafar sat so impotently in Dehli and the deposed Sikh infant Maharaja Dulip Singh was entertained at exotic parties in London, the British East India Company was able to establish a new over-riding Ruling Body under the Governor-General and Supreme Commander. Punjab being the latest acquisition was first of all entrusted to a three-member Board of administration with Headquarter at Lahore. The first members were Lawrence brothers and Robert Montgomery with Mr. P. Melwill as Secretary. They set up Board's offices in the Residency, which happened to be the existing Chief Secretary's block in the Punjab Civil Secretariat, with clerical office in the adjoining tomb of Anarkali. In 1853, Punjab was made a Chief Commissioner's province. The institutional arrangements were streamlined. Proper departments came into being with financial and Judicial Commissioners, the Chief Secretary, a Secretariat at Provincial level, which had of course evolved on the nucleus of the Board's Secretariat at Lahore. The institution of Divisional Commissioners, Deputy Commissioners, Divisional Judges, extra Assistant Commissioner, the Courts and Jails Department were set up. Not only that a fulfledged Education Inspectorate, Irrigation department, Industries and Organizations for development of minerals and settlement operations throughout the Punjab were attended to on priority basis, they also started working in other fields-in respect of Railway, Roads, Bridges, Transport and Navigation etc. The work of territories under the Province of Punjab increased with passage of time and for better administrative control it was given under the charge of Lt. Governor in the year 1859. Since then various Governors remained posted and worked towards achievement of exploiting resources and more control on the locals. The administrative system followed was like any other province of India. Lahore was made the Provincial headquarters of newly acquired territories including Frontier. The Governor's office and Civil Secretariat were located here and all the administrative divisions and districts were controlled from here. A well-planned cantonment was built and army, public and other agencies had also established their headquarters at

Lahore. This privilege of the city led to automatic expansion and development institutions on the pattern of British policies.

One of the most important works undertaken by the Board of Administration at a very early stage was the excavation of the Bari Doab Canal, to a branch of which Lahore is indebted for its irrigation. This marked the commencement of the canal works throughout the Province which converted Punjab deserts into smiling fields and added incalculable sums to the wealth of the people. They brought prosperity to hundreds of thousands and fortunes to many, particularly in connection with the exports of wheat and cotton. Every year they rendered possible the cultivation of wheat and cotton worth millions of sterling. Throughout 2,450 miles of main canals, 1,650 miles of branches and 12,700 miles of distributaries had been dug out to irrigate the million of acres for crops. The success of these gigantic undertakings induced the Government to put its hand to one still more gigantic task, known as the Triple Canal Project. The first drew upon the Jhelum and was to throw the water of that river into the Chenab irrigating 345,000 acres on its way. The Chenab, thus reinforced, would be able not only to supply the vast irrigation works already dependent on it, but also feed a second unit of the triple system. Thus, the Upper Chenab Canal, of which the Viceroy, Lord Harding, opened the headworks in April 1912, was to irrigate 650,000 acres and carry its surplus waters into the Ravi. The third unit of the system, the Lower Bari Doab Canal, was then to be taken out on the south of the Ravi the combined waters of the three rivers and irrigate 78,000 acres, all lying waste upto Multan, manly covering the "Ganji Bar" tract.

While changes were being made in the Punjab, they did not neglect the city of Lahore. "To improve the ventilation" the city walls were cut down from 30 to 15 feet in height and finally removed in 1881, the gates only being left standing. Moreover the moat and the uneven ground surrounding it were levelled in 1863-1864 and made into a garden which was much appreciated by the citizens. The population, which in 1849 was about 95,000 and in 1881 was 157, 287, increased enormously and many people now lived outside the original circuit of the walls." This caused emergence of new colonies, with large and most modern homes with change in architectural patterns.

The vicinities of Lahore were best described by Sir John Lawrence:- "Few suburban localities could be found in any Province presenting such peculiar sanitary difficulties as the vicinity of Lahore. The station of Anarkali with its adjuncts is scattered over an area of several square miles, over which extend the ruins of not one but of several successive cities of various eras and various dynasties. The surface of this extraordinary plain is diversified by mounds, kilns, bricks, stones, broken masses of masonry, decaying structures, hollows, excavations, and all the debris of habitations that have passed away. The soil is sterile and impregnated with saltpetre, but the ground is intersperced with vegetation, and though generally arid, yet from its undulating nature, possesses an unfortunate aptitude for the accumulation of stagnant water." The whole of this had gradually been levelled and it proved a valuable quarry for the supply of brick metal for railways and roads and of materials for the construction of modern improvements by the British in the city. The establishment of Central Museum, the Mayo School of Arts the Chief Court of Lahore, Lawrence Montgomery Hall, the Government College, the District Court, the Mayo Hospital, the Railway Station of Lahore, Judicial Commissioner's office and many other buildings with most appropriate designing were added which brought out the population from walled city and laid foundations of Modern Lahore. The Gothic Colonial architecture using mostly the indigenous material, in land-mark and out-stands the old structure in the walled city except the Mughal Monuments.

Special efforts towards the improvement of Lahore were made during the Lieutenant-Governorhsip of Sir Charles Rivaz who took particular interest in the development of the Capital. It was under his orders that a broad metalled road with grass borders and side paths replaced the dusty abomination which formerly constituted the Mall. He gave Lahore new buildings not unworthy of their predecessors, the University Hall, the new Accountant-General's office, the Public Works Secretariat, the Administrative offices of the North-Western Railway, the Clerks' Colony near Chauburji, the officer's colony Riwaz Garden (now replaced by private modern Bunglaws) and the fine overhead-Bridge, (Garhi Shahu Bridge), replaced last year by Muhammad Shahbaz Sharif, Chief Minister Punjab, which carries across the railway line and driving towards Shalamar. He first installed electric light in the streets of Lahore city and improved and extended the Agri-Horticultural Garden adjoining Lawrence Garden as well as the Zoo, which is well worth a visit if only to admire the beautiful white peacocks and pheasants. The earthquake of 1905 did much damage to many historic buildings in Lahore, including Wazir Khan's Mosque and the Montgomery Hall. Not only did Sir Charles repair these damages but he co-operated with Lord Curzon in his restoration of the Mughal buildings in the Fort and of the mausoleum of Jahangir and its Serai.

It is interesting to note how the centre of the civil station had, with the improvement of sites at a distance from the city, moved continuously further and further south. In the day of the Board of Administration the President lived in the present Punjab Civil Secretariat, next door to Anarkali's tomb, and his offices and staff had houses behind and around it. Sir John Lawrence as Chief commissioner lived beyond the Chauburji. The Lower Mall and the Gol Bagh were then in the fashionable quarter. In 1859, however, the occupation by Sir Robert Montgomery of the present Government House commenced the move southward. During the Lieutenant-Governorship of Sir Donald MacLeod the civil station moved out to what was then known as Donald Town the locality developing on the Mall around Bedan Road and behind Regal Cinema. Some of the earlier shops were at this period built on the present Upper Mall. In late years housing expanded and moved still further south and Donald Town and the Upper Mall were now entirely given up to official and commercial business. Government House became the centre of the residential quarter of today but this spreads a considerable distance around. The tendency to move south was exemplified by the Punjab Club which in 1906 left its old quarters and built its fine premises (now Pakistan Administrative Staff College Building) next door to Government House on the Mian Mir side. It was probably thereafter that Government built a number of residences for its officers still further south, on the site which adjoined the Race-course and extended to the canal. This area is now called GOR-I.

Times changed from the 1870s when landlords were shy of building and officers could get accommodation only by buying their houses and trusting to recoup themselves by their sale when they left the Station. The expansions in the executive and legislative departments of Government, the strengthening of the Chief Court, the increased establishment that was required to control Irrigation Buildings and Roads Department with a charge so extensive and wide-spread as that of the present day, and, in particular, the extraordinary growth of trade and commerce and of the departments which dealt with canal irrigation, railways, posts and telegraphs, year by year brought more residents to the city of Lahore.

A campaign by Government was launched to introduce local products to Europe and England especially the raw materials, for this all the offices were instructed to survey, collect data and communicate. Sometime Museums were considered the best mode to use as lever to find out the raw wealth. A comparison of the four exhibitions were held in Lahore which marks the progress of the province and its Capital as a centre of all Government sponsored activities. The first such exhibition of products and raw material was held in 1864 in the defunct building of Tolinton Market, which provided ample accommodation for all the exhibits then procurable. The second exhibition was held in 1881 in the buildings which was then completed for the Mayo School of Art. The exhibition building of 1864 was at that time used as a Museum but as the collections increased more room became necessary and was provided in the block in which the Museum is now housed. The third exhibition was opened in this new Museum in 1893. For the fourth exhibition, opened by Sir Louis Dane in December 1909, it was found necessary to erect special buildings on the spacious open ground to the north of the Fort. A feature of this exhibition was the great part taken by the non-official agencies which organised it. The section that illustrated the development of canal irrigation in the Punjab, and the excellent arrangements made for the amusements of the large crowds of visitors with wrestling matches and other national sports, were particularly noticeable. It was later decided to convert the site of the exhibition into a public park called after Lord Minto, the Viceroy of India. After partition it was named Iqbal Park and a 'Yadgar' or monument called Minar Pakistan was built here. Although some of the area has been encroached yet in the noisy and haphazardly expanding city, it is still a park and a big relief for walled city residents.

It would be tedious to recount in detail the progress of Lahore since the annexation. Its steps might be marked by the dates of the various fine buildings which one after the other have added to its dignity. These are in many cases associated with the visits of distinguished guests whom Lahore has had the privilege of entertaining and who were attracted by the importance of the Lahore and the unique interest of its old memorials. We have already seen that Lord Lawrence, when Viceroy, visited Lahore in 1864. His successor, Lord Mayo, came to Lahore in 1870 and presided at a farewell banquet to Sir Donald MacLeod when he relinquished the Lieutenant Governorship after holding it for six months more than the usual period of five years. In 1870 Lahore welcomed the first of her royal visitors in the person of the late Duke of Edinburgh. He was followed in 1876 by his brother the Prince of Wales, afterwards the late King-Emperor Edward the seventh. This visit was remarkable for the assembly of Punjab Chiefs who came to do homage and were accommodated in magnificent camps on the open ground to the north of the Fort. In 1879 Lord Lytton held a memorable review here, and in 1886 Lord Dufferin came to Lahore when Lady Dufferin laid the foundation stone of the Aitchison Hospital for Women. Next year Lord Lansdowne followed his predecessor and opened the Forman Christian College. Lords Elgin, Curzon, Minto and Harding, during the course of their viceroyalties, all visited Lahore and their visits were the occasion of appropriate collaboration ceremonies. The year 1890 is memorable for the visit of the late Prince Albert Victor who attended a great cavalry camp at Muridke and on the 3rd February laid the foundation stone of the museum which was built partly in commemoration of Queen Victoria's first Jubilee: another building associated with her Jubilee is the Town Hall commenced in 1887, and this was opened by the Prince. King-Emperor George the fifth, when Prince of Wales, together with the Princess of Wales, (Queen Mary), visited Lahore with their presence in 1905. This visit was signalized by another splendid assemblage of Punjab Chiefs and by the ardent expressions of loyalty with which the people evidenced their attachment to the crown. Among other royal visitors have been the Czar Nicolas II (then the Czarewitch) in 1891 and the Crown Prince of Prussia in 1910. The Amir of Afghanistan was also entertained in 1907.

The period after 1910 brought in more political consciousness to the Lahore. The brief history comprised in the preceding page is an attempt to describe the fortunes of Lahore from its foundation by Loh to 1920s. It is true that its old buildings do not carry us far back into the past. But they are excellent specimens of the taste and architecture of the Mughals during the seventeenth and eighteenth centuries. We have lost much of the work of this period which would have been as interesting as that which has survived. We have to regret the loss inflicted on Lahore by the wars and turbulence which mark its history and the tendency which makes each passing generation heedless of its predecessor's works, unconscious that its successors will be equally heedless, and intent only on leaving new records of their own making. More keen is our regret at the irretrievable losses inflicted by Sikhs by sheer vandalism such as that which, in the early years of the British administration, allowed the destruction of old buildings for the sake of the bricks. Fortunately a more enlightened policy removed all fear for the future. The Government now treats its inheritance with reverence and is taking care to what has come down to it. Lahore is thus a city which not only attract those who are interested in memorials of the past but also is a centre of official, business, educational and social life second to none in Pakistan. Moreover, the conditions under which it may be visited are as pleasant and as comfortable as can be found anywhere in the East. It would now be of interest to mention the role the British Bureaucracy and traders played in general.

The English who had entered as Traders transformed their entity into imperial policemen of the British Crown. They lavishly enjoyed their Indian empire with all pomp and show whether it was the camel back, in palanquins or the elephant howdhas. It sometimes appeared to be more than a theatrical display. Their supremacy apparently oriental, inherited from Mughals was intended to overawe the indigenous and give the Company's employees a proper sense of their own authority. Shortly after complete subjugation the Indian people found them benevolent and impressive always adjustable. Proper Secretariat, offices of the Commissioners and Deputy Commissioners and other departmental units sprang up for city of Lahore. The Governor House took the shape of a policy planning cell and things started moving in the direction, these are working today. The Police and Army control was more stringent and the law and order enforcement strict to any extent. In 1857 there was revolt by Indian population against their established Victorian Over lords. This was, however, branded as sepoy mutiny by the British. The local administration took measures for disarming the native soldiers. As far as Lahore was concerned the British forces were located at two places, the Lahore Fort and Mian Mir Cantt. The military establishment located at Anarkali Cantt. had already been moved out to Mian Mir, as due to some epidemic Many British soldiers had died. The native soldiers were disarmed. On 29th June, 1858 two men of 35th native Infantry were blown from guns on the Anarkali parade ground by sentence of drum-head, court martialled for sedition and intended mutiny. Some petty events also took place where the guilty were punished with five years rigorous imprisonment. Needless to detail that the British protective measures were successful and there was no rebellion in Lahore. In the year 1858 India was transferred from East India

Company. to the British Crown. The old Mughal King Bahadur Shah Zafar exiled to Burma. The Punjab became one of the provinces of Indian Nominal-changes such as Governor General into Viceroy and Chief Commissioner as Lt. Governor. This political change in the fate of Lahore embodied another subtle change in the life style of the rulers and the ruled. The British trading community turned into eastern land barons in an Indian paradise. They enjoyed the local exotic company of Nawabs, dancing girls and courtesans scans. It was not the British who were discovering a new and a fascinating world, the Punjabis and specially Lahoris were simultaneously viewing and absorbing the strange mannerism and customs of white skinned newcomers. The locals experimented with new modes of tailoring and unusual fashions which soon out-did the British in the elegance of their western dressing. The dress of Indian women also went under small striking changes. Meanwhile, the India in general and Lahore in particular was gradually being re-shaped under the influence of the British. New buildings sprang up on almost every corner and old managements were re-fashioned to serve the new requirements of the administration. Sometimes tanks were filled and transferred into tennis courts and tombs and turrets modified to house clerical establishment. Once the British had established, the old city of Lahore also received its share of changes. The British filled the ditch surrounding the old city and sculpted into a massive circular garden. This was the beginning of the century of British renovation which was to transform Lahore to a western style locality. Sometimes the new places and landscaping were carried out without any regard of sensitivity to the indigenous design but the over all impression was that mostly the repairs, trees and lawns and architecture were welcomed by the locals. Gradually Lahore re-emerged as a city that she had been of old. From southern side of old city the new rulers laid a long special boulevard which they called the Mall. This wide, well-man-cared thoroughfare connected old Lahore with newly set up military cantonment on the east (Mian Mir) and around its across the authorities built their civil lines. The new Lahore was taking shape and once again had important cross roads especially in front of (Now) the WAPDA House. The cross roads here nick-named with Charing Cross. By the early 20th century Lahore was in its Prime. The new colonial architecture befittingly gave a picturesque look to the city. It was cloaked in spacious lawns, luxuriant shade trees, and there was presence of an order and harmony and all this left the old Citadel dooming in the background.

As one travels east up the Mall, today, one by one the British structures reveal themselves, the Town Hall, the Central Museum. Kim's gun, College of Arts the Zamzamah, the High Court, the Cathedral, and the General Post Office. There were dozens of shops, and Faletti's hotel, where the smart and the affluent stayed during the winter (social) season. Then further up Empress Road is the great railroad station-the hub of the city's activity. Here the Khyber Mail still arrives, and the Express still hurtles south towards Karachi. The Government

House, set amongst beautiful gardens with breathtaking beds of vibrant flowers, tranquil stretches of trees and lush green lawns, was not far from the Gymkhana Club, which looked out over the race course. The Punjab Club looked like a military academy, while Chief's College or 'Aitchison' looks like a Maharaj's palace, its red domes and ornate extrances set above the green hedges and trees. And at the end of this esplanade ran the Canal (now fed differently), one of the lined with willows and flowering trees, the canal provided a cool place for a leisurely stroll.

But aside from preserving monuments to the city's past, the British Governors who ruled the Punjab from Lahore in five years terms (each) also attempted to maintain and foster the cultural life of the city, they used as their base. They held annual exhibitions of local industrial arts, and erected public libraries as well as hospitals. But their most notable contribution to the life of the city lies in the numerous educational institutions they founded there. For example, the year of 1882 alone saw the completion of the Mayo School of Arts, a Veterinary school dedicated to developing better horse breeding, and a technical institute established in honour of the Queen's jubilee. Their stellar achievement in this field, however, is the Lahore Orintal College, Government College, which started out as a non-degree awarding institution, and then later blossomed into the University of the Punjab. This institution, which in truth was initially proposed by the local Punjab Government and pushed to fruition by the Anjuman-i-Punjab, was designed by the British regents to perform two primary functions: first, it was intended to foster the diffusion of Western literature into the Punjabi vernacular, and in so doing to bring the European classics to the Indians, and second, to promote generally the 'enlightended study of Eastern classical languages'. The excitement generated by this project catalysed its development from a mere proposal in 1858 to a full-fledged university in 24 years. Shortly after that, the Chief's College was established for the sons of ruling chiefs and other prominent men.

This British emphasis on education and the diffusion of Western ideas, though intended to produce generations of useful, articulate celrks, produced as well something wholly unexpected: the gestation of Western democratic ideas which would eventually lead to the eloquent rejection of the Government which introduced them. By the late 1850s, when Queen Victoria had declared herself 'Empress of India' and it had become de rigeur for members of the royal house – such as Prince Albert Victor of Wales in 1890- to ride imperially through the streets of Lahore on the back of an elephant and be entertained with dinner parties at Shalamar Gardens, the first waves of organised revolt were already surging.

One may not ignore the indirect implications of western education system. It made conscious the common man indirectly through the media, the curriculm and European literature about rights of the common man and obligations of the Government. It infact made aware the people of the good Governance which was due from the rulers and to reduce the exploitation to the minimum level. The Local Government institutions although originally designed for smooth functioning of the administration made aware the man in the street about his participation and role in the Government through various Local Government tiers. Thus awareness taken at a larger level throughout the country levelled ground for founding the political parties and the beginning came in the shape of founding of Congress in Bengal which was followed by inititation of similar proceedings for Muslim League formation in Dacca in 1906. This also created a demand for self rule, more participation, seats in Assemblies, adult franchise, more share in civil services and reduction in the level of exploitation of resources i.e. from raw material producing country to an industrial society itself. These developments had the obvious effect on the city of Lahore which was the capital of Punjab and any activity would mean activity of the Province. When the Muslim and Hindus parted their ways and Muslims voted for leadeship of Quaid-e-Azam, Lahore was the centre of Muslim politics i.e. Muslim League activities originated in Lahore city. Our national poet Dr. Muhammad Iqbal floated idea of a separate State at Allahabad session of Muslim League. Conventions and meeting were held in Lahore. There were number of rallies, conferences and public meetings by other national parties as well. The Lahore was the only city which took lead in respect of political activities by the Muslim Women in the sub-continent. They held their rallies separately and voiced their support and demand for separate homeland for Muslims. Finally it was Lahore where the Pakistan Resolution was passed on 23rd March, 1940. It was the famous parade ground of Ranjit Singh, Cricket and Polo ground of British, Minto Park of the late 20s where Pakistan Muslim League held its stormy session which was attended by Quaid-e-Azam Muhammad Ali Jinnah, Sher-e-Bengal Maulvi A. K. Fazal ul Haq including all note-worthy Muslim League leaders from all over India that the formal and final resolution for a separate State under the name and banner of "Pakistan" was passed at the park, now known as Iqbal Park or Yadgar-e-Pakistan.

The Lahoris never lagged behind participating in the protest rallies and they suffered bitterly at the hands of the administration whether it was Home Rule Movement or the Pakistan rally. Finally after emergence of Pakistan in August 1947 it was the city of Lahore which welcomed the largest number of immigrants who had been pushed by the India into Pakistan. The Lahoris welcomed their brethren and shared their agony. In very poor and appalling economic conditions without any finances Government machinery and resources, Lahore, welcomed and accommodated the victims of the biggest ever migration in the world history. Till their settlement, and establishment of a formal machinery for running affairs of the state Lahore remained the centre of activities of Pakistan. National reconstruction work was planned and executed by the administrators and volunteers, in Lahore. Then came the formal phase of political Governments which was taken in hands by the Muslim League and in subsequent years by other parties. Lahore was declared capital of the Province of Punjab. It continued to serve that purpose till 1955 when it was declared capital of West Pakistan. The then Pakistan State had two wings. East Pakistan with its capital at Dacca and West Pakistan had four provinces which were merged into one Unit in 1955 with one Assembly to sit and work at Lahore. Lahore continued to host the affairs of all the provinces as one unit, until the catastrophe of 1971 led by India tore apart the Eastern wing. It was thereafter, that the one unit was dismembered and Lahore reverted back as capital of the Province of Punjab. The work of Provincial reconstruction started afresh with full vigour and enthusiasm. From civilian Martial Law imposed by the Peoples Party to the final march towards return of democracy and other such historical movements were witnessed by this city. The Muslim League Government returned in office in year 1991 led by Mian Nawaz Sharif and again in the year 1997 as Prime Minister of Pakistan with a heavy mandate. The city received a big development boost and new era of reconstruction and Development of Lahore has since started. The roads are being widened, the squatters being thrown out, parks and gardens being restored and new and more welfare institutions being strengthened.

After Independence the city of Lahore's character changed from its secular social set up to a purely Muslim city. The immigration brought in a big influx of the immigrants which disturbed the housing fabric already planned during the British Authorities. There was a continuous shift of population from rural areas in general and Lahore came under pressure on its existing resources. The housing sector turned into a surging sea of haphazard growth in all directions outside the walled city which merely appeared as an island. All this development for many years (until recently) remained basically ill-planned without care for hygiene and other basic facilities. The housing localities were partly developed by private sector which in case of well off would take the shape of a colony and in case of poor and low income would be termed as Kachi Abadi. There is no count of Kachi Abadis which sometimes, are also called slums. The Government realizing the intensity of problem had to set up an organization in the name of Lahore Improvement Trust and later Lahore Development Authority to regulate the housing and other amenities. It is, however, unfortunate that so far they have neither been able to make public the Master Plan of the Lahore city nor control the ill expanding private colonies. The first area which got a modern housing project after 1947, was the Gulberg. Later the localities of Samanabad, Garden Town, Muslim Town, Shah Jamal, Shadman, Allama Iqbal Town, Anguri Bagh Scheme, Shad Bagh, in addition to low income housing projects like Township, Green Town, localities on Ferozepur Road, around Multan Road, Bund Road, Iqbal Town and Jauhar Town, emerged. The latest addition of a planned private housing is the Defence Society, where land was acquired on cheep rates and sold on market price. It is the planned and posh locality with all amenities. The tendency was and persists that whenever an area was developed for housing sector the adjoining lands were purchased and sold by property dealers for private housings and these would automatically become a burden on the sewerage and other public health facilities. Besides these the civil servants and employees in private sector had their own housing societies which also developed a number of colonies such as Revenue Society, Judicial Society, PCSIR Society, Income Tax Society, TECH Society, Canal View Housing Society etc. etc. A recent trend by the investers is the purchase of land at commercially viable points and developing them into multi-storyed plazas and sell out on huge profits. Such plazas are seen in and around Gulberg locality and flat system in Cantonment colonies and those developed hut type accommodation by purchasing old big houses. We know that while the population was around 1,90,000 in 1898 it has swollen to about 80 lacs in 1999. Accordingly there is pressure on the resources, facilities and in terms of supply and demand on utilities.

In addition to the unruly growth of housing, Lahore has also become an industrial city where Government promoted and set up proper industrial sectors with facilities of infrastructure. From steel furnaces to textile and chemical plants and hosiery the industrial sector has awfully encircled the city. From Lahore to Gujranwala and Sheikhpura on the north the city is linked with these two towns with countless industrial units and factories, the same is the situation on the Multan Road where due to industrial estate in Chunian not an inch of land is vacant on the National Highway. The same way industrial plants are touching the border of Kasur City. These industrial areas again have their labour force who have their labour colonies and thus an additional burden on the city's ill-planned and insufficient scarce resources.

The city has advanced in many other ways and became an educational centre of the Province with countless number of Intermediate Colleges, High Schools, Colleges of Women and men in almost all the localities whereas before partition there used to be only Government College, Islamia College and Dyal Singh College. The Lahore city has now an Engineering University, three Medical Colleges and a University known as Lahore University of Management Sciences, in private sector. The mushroom growth of Computer Colleges, Business Institutions and centres for Management Sciences are found almost on every main road who privately impart instructions and have their affiliation with Universities abroad. The Punjab University which was established in the year 1882 fell short of space and was shifted to a big open area around the canal towards Niaz Baig and Jauhar Town side. The University has an American style campus, many hostels with beautiful locations on both sides of the canal bank.

With the increase in population and expansion of the city there emerged a need for accommodation and catering facilities for the visitors. Before partition there were only one or two hotels including Falettis which were considered of some standard. Somehow the private sector is now managing at least three 5-star hotels in the city. These are Pearl Continental, Avari and Holiday Inn. In addition to this smaller hotels, well furnished in various localities like Gulberg, Faisal Town, Lower Mall, are catering to the needs of the incoming visitors and tourists. In the absence of not many cultural and entertainment facilities, eating out has become a fashion in modern localities and families come out in the evenings and rush to the popular places like Chinese hotels, Tikka Kabab shops and those preparing traditional spicy food items of old Lahore which are now found in almost all the localities.

Another sector which is being given top priority by the present Government is the development of roads and public transport facilities. The city of Lahore has been linked with the Motor-Way and Government is pursuing a big campaign for widening metalled roads in the city by removing unauthorised and squatters,. A big headway had really been made by the Chief Minister in his tenure as he personally monitored these mostly and insisted to maintain a standard and minimum quality. Shahbaz Sharif was a workaholic. He held meeting of executing agencies and officers at site e.g. if a road is being built he will spend hours early morning and check the digging, drainage and carpeting before the traffic resumes and world like to see that the work was done in three shifts, round the clock. He was getting this work done through Army. Similarly the public transport system is being improved. The availability of taxis which had totally extinguished during the last few years was revived which not only provided jobs but also facilitated the movement of passengers. It was given out by the authorities that before the year is out a compact transport system will be in operation in the city and comfortable busses will be available to common-man for travelling within the city on reasonable fares. Private sector is being offered incentives to invest as public run cooperatives have inflicted heavy losses to the public exchequer.

In Lahore of pre-partition days only Mayo Hospital and a couple of Corporation dispensaries were available to the residents which have since multiplied with the Government patronage. The Mayo Hospital itself has been expanded at least five times with separate hospital units for orthopedics, nuclear medicine, ophthalmology and cancer units in addition to may other disciplines. Ganga Ram Hospital set up by Sir Ganga Ram as a dispensary has been developed into s Women Medical College with health facilities at a much larger scale. The college of community medicines, Allama Iqbal Medical College, Nawaz Sharif Social Security Hospital, Multan Road, Services Hospital, Lahore General Hospital, Ithefaq Hospital, Sharif Medical city, Mian Munshi Hospital and Mian Nawaz Sharif Hospital in Farooq Ganj locality and Children Hospital Ferozpur Road are some of the major hospitals which provide health care. In addition to this there are hundred of clinics and Laboratories run by private investors which treat from ordinary accidents to Heart Surgery with countless number of small Polly Test Clinics.

Lahore was known to be a city of gardens which characteristically went under change with political upheavals. Sometime one could see gardens and sometimes ruins. When the British occupied they vandalised with old buildings and monuments, already exploited by the Sikhs for purpose of bricks etc. but also developed a couple of parks for hygiene of the city and its residents. This included especially the garden around the walled city, Botanical Garden on the Mall, Lawrence Garden and Race Course Park etc. etc. As already mentioned, somehow this remained ignored for quite sometime and it was during the last decade or so that efforts at Government level were made to save the green spots and add new ones. Those whose names can be specially mentioned include General Ghulam Jilani Khan, the late Governor of Punjab who was keenly interested in the establishment of such parks. Those constructed in his period include Lahore Park on Raiwind Road, Jallo Park on the left bank of Lahore Canal, Model Town Park, and Gulshan-e-Iqbal Park. Later on Nawaz Sharif added Lienear in place of 'China Basti' on Ferozpur Road, Iqbal Park (renovated) Forest Park and a couple of spots in the city. The major operation these days going on is to lay a garden around the old city by removing unauthorised markets, houses and shops again under occupation of squatters which will certainly restore the green grandeur of Lahore. Infact Nawaz Sharif picked up the thread and accomplished all the beautification of Lahore. He saw the accomplishment of Cultural Complex of the city and a permanent Art Gallery at Ferozepur Road. General Ghulam Jilani ordered taking over the Race Course and made a beautiful park with a Lake and jogging tracks. The restoration of Bara Dari of Kamran, in the river Ravi, and garden around was also done by Nawaz Sharif the then Chief Minister.

SOME MONUMENTS OF THE CITY

THE MAUSOLEUM OF DATA GANJ BAKHSH

THE PATRON SAINT OF LAHORE

Outside Bhati Gate of the old (walled) city, to the west of Circular Road, is the celebrated mausoleum of Hazrat Data Ganj Bakhsh, "the saint, the bestower of treasure." His real name is "Ali Makhdum, Hujweri, of Ghazni. His father's name was Usman, son of Ali Jalabi Ghaznavi, and he was a disciple of Sheikh Abul Fazl bin Hassan Khutbi. He, it is said followed the arms of Masud, the son and successor of Mahumd Ghaznvi, to Lahore where he settled to preach Islam in 431 A. H. (1039 A.D.) Having lived thirty-four years in Lahore, during which time he conferred great benefits on the people by his learning and piety, he died in 465 A.H. (1072 A.D.), and was buried close to the mosque which he had himself built. The mausoleum was constructed by Sultan Ibrahim, a successor of Masud. Ali Makhdum Hujweri was an eminent scholar, and was the author of many books on theology and religion. Khwaja Moin-ud-Din Chishti, the celebrated saint of Ajmere, passed forty days of seclusion and meditation at the tomb of Data Ganj Bakhsh, and after the period was over, he was, it is said, deeply affected by the graces showered upon him at this holy place, and he repeated the following verse standing at the foot of the tomb out of respect for the saint:-

"The bestower of treasure (Ganj Bakhsh) in both worlds, reflector of the splendour of God,

An accomplished spiritual guide for the learned and a guide for the ignorant."

From the date the saint of Ghazni came to be called Ganj Bakhsh, the couplet is inscribed over the doorway of the tomb. Maulana Jami, in his Nafahat-ul-Uns and Dara Shikoh, in his Safinat-ul-Aulia, speak in high terms of the accomplishments of Data Ganj Bakhsh as a religious preceptor, and from the times of the Ghaznivide kings up to the present day his memory has been held in the greatest veneration by all classes of people. He was a great author of his time, and among other works he wrote a book called the Kashf-ul-Mahjub, or "The Revelation of the Hidden." A fair is held at the tomb each Thursday, which is, as always, largely attended by the faithful.

The floor of the entrance to the mausoleum, and the door frames, as well as the platforms to the right and left of it, are of marble. This is the work of

Emperor Akbar. Over the old entrance gateway on a slab of marble the following verses of the celebrated poet Maulana Abdul Rehman Jami are inscribed:-

"God is excellent,"

"There is no God but God, and Muhammad (PUH) is the Prophet of God."

"This mausoleum, the foundation of which was laid through the bounty of God,

Is intended as sepulchre for Makhdum Ali, who has joined the Divine essence.

Having departed from this transient world, he obtained eternal life;

Therefore the pre-eminent date of his death was found in the word Hast (ever existent)"

There is a small receptacle for water on the floor to the north of the tomb. The devotees take this water as a sacred object to their homes for the sake of obtaining benedictions, and apply it to their eyes to benefit their souls.

The locality adjoining to the mausoleum of Data Ganj Bakhsh is known as Shish Mahal, from the palace of mirrors which existed here in the time of the Muhammaden Emperors.

The mausoleum is highly popular with the residents of Pakistan of all classes. The anniversary of the death of the saint is celebrated on 20th Safar, when a great fair is held at the shrine. Maharaja Ranjit Singh, who held the saint in great reverence, used to make an offering of one thousand rupees on the date of the Urs, or the anniversary of death. Maharani Chand Kour, wife of Maharaja Kharak Singh and mother of Nao Nihal Singh, built a vaulted chamber in this mausoleum in 1895 Samvat, and Ranjit Singh himself had it periodically repaired.

Among the most interesting object of the mausoleum are the ancient manuscript Qurans, presented by different Kings and Nawabs of Hindustan, which are preserved to this day and are on display in the recently set up Gallery. Most of these are excellent specimens of the art of calligraphy.

Many changes have taken place since the original tomb was constructed.

Author of ten or more books the saint is best known for his Kashf-ul-Mahjub, Revelation of the Unseen called "the oldest Persian treatise on Sufism" by Prof. R. A. Nicholson in his early 1911 English translation. This magnum opus provides a complete system of Sufism. The book and its translations, in several languages, continue to be read by scholars, aspirant sufis and the common man. Widely venerated in South Asia, Hazrat Data Ganj Bakhsh, 'Bestower of Favours', he, is the patron saint of Lahore.

The mosque he built and his modest tomb have attracted devotees about one thousand years. People from all walks of life and religious persuasions continue to come to pay homage. On the site of the original mosque, a new mosque was built in 1279 A. H. (1826 A.D) with a chamber topped by a dome. Later repairs were carried out by one Jhando. In 1340 A. H. /1921 A. D. Mian Ghulam Rasool Khathwala rebuilt this mosque. In 1342 A. H./1923 A. D. a tank was built for ablution in the south side of the old mosque while a double-storey chamber was built for the call to prayer. Later the tank and the minaret were demolished. This mosque was periodically damaged by the floods of the river Ravi.

The Punjab Government under order of Muhammad Nawaz Sharif, Prime Minister of Pakistan has greatly extended the campus of the Data Sahib complex. Apparently an effort has been made to blend the design with architectural feature of the mausoleum. This gives a slightly familiar look of our indigenous architecture instead of Minar of Turkish style generally followed in Istanbul. A brochure issued by the Auqaf Department has details of the Phase wise completion of the constructions. According to this:-

"The earliest available visual record of this building is that by the Lahore artist Miran Bukhsh Moortanwaley (1877-194), who lived in Kucha Musawaran of Gumti Bazar in the walled city of Lahore. With miniature-style meticulousness, the painting owes a great deal to the Company School and modeling of figures. The mausoleum depicted is an octagonal marble structure with perforated screens in the Mughal style and a green dome. To its west stands a mosque, now not with one but five domes. The red sandstone patterns on the façade and the ribbed white domes speak for the growing importance of this site and the increasing veneration in which the mausoleum was held. Figures in the foreground testify that it was frequented as a centre of pilgrimage. Interestingly, there is no Ghulam Gardsih/ circumambulatory space, around the dome that exists at present. The addition of the circumambulatory space in matching white marble underlines the growing commitment of the Lahoris who proudly refer to Lahore as "Data di Nagri", the Bestower's City". Considerable changes have continued to be made to the Mosque and peripheral buildings in different times. The gates have reconstructed many a times. The place of allocations changed. One of the gates with gold and glass work was donated by Shah of Iran. The workmanship is superb and was installed by Prime Minister of Pakistan."

The Provincial Auqaf Department took over the management of "Data Darbar" on November 1, 1960. The then existing mosque which was damaged by storm and earthquake and consequently a need was felt for the new mosque as also an expansion in the surrounding area for visitors, and the faithful especially the Langer Khana etc. which posed problems during the 'Urs Days' and Thursdays. The people also faced lot of problem during Ramzan, on Juma prayers. In the late Seventies plans for the extension of mosque began. The, late, President General Zia ul-Haq laid the foundation stone of the new Mosque on 28th January, 1978. The Committee selected a design inspired by Thatta's Shah Mosque, Lahore's Badshahi Mosque and the Green Mosque of Turkey in 1980 after an international competition. The construction commenced in the middle of 1982 and was completed in 1989. This phase of the mosque spread over 1,60,00-sft. was formally inaugurated on 28th November, 1989 by the Chief Minister Punjab Mian Muhammad Nawaz Sharif.

The work on Phase-II of Data Darbar remained pending for almost 7 years. When the work restarted in March 1997, the basement was a garbage dump. After about two year, 3,00,000 sft. built up area was added along-with parking the shops removed for a Samaa Hall. In addition there is Langer-khana, charity kitchen, ablution areas for men and women, offices, gallery for historic relics and a library etc. This expansion has only been possible with the Punjab Government active help acquiring in land, under Building.

The top, main, floor reflects the most dramatic transformation. The original design for the remaining portion was a repetition of the bulbous arcade of Phase-I.

According to Government version they have done a lot in the expansion and beautification of structure keeping in view the central Theme and Lay out of original tomb Arches and the "Ghulam Gardush". It is yet to be seen as to how the expansion, which was at a big cost, meets the needs of faithful and the visitors. Providing glass domes and 'Chahar Bagh' beauty is not the need of the commoner who visits Data Sahib. They many aesthetically look nice but the visitor needs space, easy space for prayers and mediation. Those visiting on Urs, during Ramzan and Fridays and a sizable number of faithful who want to stay at the premises when they want to enjoy the company of the saint to relish the spiritual stance.

THE BARADARI OF MIRZA KAMRAN

This very substantial old edifice, with its magnificent, high arches once stood, on the right bank of the Ravi in the centre of a garden in early 16the century, a triumph of engineering art. For more than one and half a century has the impetuous current of the ancient Ravi struggled to annihilate its walls, whose feet it washes, but, with the exception of a portion washed away at a time beyond the memory of the living generation, the edifice stands quite unaffected by the ebb and flow of the river. It is now in the centre of the River Ravi. Prime Minister Nawaz Sharif, when Chief Minister had got built a strong embankment around the Baradari, which was also restored. The water tank and fountains were also put in order and the garden towards west re-shaped to some extent. A restaurant was also built and horticulture improved. It was given to the Punjab Tourism Development Corporation who have the boats etc. stationed on the left bank. The visitors, who are mostly local tourists hire motor boat and usually go to the Baradari for picnics. While ordinarily the river Ravi, now diverted by India is dry, it is only in rainy season, that the river could overflow and damage. The monument has been saved from this too by provision of this strong defence of stone embankment. The building of Baradari is made of solid masonry, and its appearance in the heart of the river is imposing and picturesque. It looks more imposing than its original location on the bank of river which must have its own grace and beauty. The founder of the first existing Mughal monument in Lahore was Mirza Kamran, son of the knightly Babar and brother of the adventurous Humayun, both founders of the Mughal Empire in Hindustan. It was situated in the midst of a beautiful garden, which was one of the earliest laid out in India by the Mughals, coming fresh from a luxuriant country abounding in verdant vegetation and rich and green gardens. The Ravi then flowed at a distance of two miles from its present bed, inasmuch as it washed the city walls. In the time of Muhammad Shah, the river having changed its course, most of the gardens laid out by the Mughal 'Omerahs' were swept away, and the garden of Mirza Kamran shared the same fate but a piece escaped which was rehabilitated to great extent by Nawaz Sharif, the then Chief Minister Punjab.

The paintings in diversified colours beneath the arches are still to be seen, as also the marks of old paths in the garden. There also exists, to the south, a portion of arched bridge work, out of which the water of fountains flowed. The edifice was used as a Rest House, a toll office, by telegraph Department during British rule and finally now in its restored shape a tourist spot. Those leaving Lahore by road get a nice view indeed, of the monument when the river is full and water repulsing during summer especially in full moonlight.

JAHANGIR'S TOMB

Emperor Jahangir ascended the throne on 10th of October 1605. Like all Mughals, Kashmir was also his favourite resort. On his last visit, while returning (from Kashmir) towards Lahore, Jahangir died near Rajauri (District Sialkot) on 27 Safar 1037, 28 October 1627, in the 58th year of his age and 23rd of his reign. His body was brought to Lahore and buried in the Dilkusha Garden of Noor Jahan. It is maintained by historians that on his death, he had expressed a wish to be buried in this garden. This also seems to have been the most likely course. The Mughals were fond of making, or at least beginning their tombs in their own life-time. Jahangir was not keeping good health for quite some time and he might have expressed his wish to be burried in the beautiful garden of his most beloved queen at Lahore, where he had spent many a happy days with her. The tomb is generally believed to have been built by Noor Jahan who was an excessively rich lady, though historian Muhammad Saleh Kambo's account unambiguously ascribed its construction to Shah Jahan. In pursuance of Emperor's will, Shah Jahan, his son and successor built the lofty mausoleum of red sandstone, measuring one hundred yards in length, round the tomb. The tomb was completed in ten years time (i.e. form 1627 to 1637), at a cost of rupees ten lacs.

The tomb is situated on the right side of the river Ravi in the suburb (of Lahore) called Shahdara. Shahdara was about three miles from Lahore city (now almost a part of Lahore) on right sight of the river Ravi, on G.T. Road, leading towards Rawalpindi. Before British occupation people reached it by boats, later by boat bridge and after 1860s with a modern rail-road bridge. During 1970s two dual carriageway, bridges, were constructed to facilitate the traffic from North to the city. The third one has now linked Lahore with Motorway. The tomb is in the centre of a Char-bagh (four-quartered garden) with the usual parkota and gateways; and causeways, water-channels and tanks arranged symmetrically around the tomb-building, to provide it with a fascinating setting. The peculiar charm of this design is that a tank with a single fountain is placed in front of each façade and each quarter also has a tank in the centre, all interconnected through a network of shallow water channels. There are, thus, eight tanks all around the tomb. Each tank has, in the middle of each side, a cascade which drains water in the canal in a beautiful way. Fountains provide inlets in them. Miniature arched bridges of brick have been made on these canals. Causeways have also been paved with brick, but it is quite likely that all these were originally made of red sandstone which seems to have been carted all the way from Fatehpur Sikri and other mines near Agra, there being no red sandstone available in the Punjab.

Tanks which are now of brick also seem to have been originally stone-cased. In fact, the tomb garden which has profuse brick work at present appears to have been originally finished in red sandstone which was plundered during Sikh rule and the present brick masonry is just the restoration work by British Archeology Department. This contention is not diluted even in the face of the fact that brick-work is a typical feature of the architecture of this region and technically, it is not impossible that these were originally built in brick itself, because those who were building it could not have borne the uneven and unplastered sight of brick-work and the style of the age demanded that these were stone-cased.

The main gateway has been provided on the western side. It is a monumental building of red sandstone, having the usual lawn portal in the central frame which is flanked by a smaller recessed wing on either side composed of double arches. White marble has been liberally used along with red sandstone in inlaid mosaic, to provide a simple yet an extremely beautiful colour combination, which was the usual scheme of finishing the ceremonial gateways from Akbar to Shah Jahan. Geometrical and stylized designs and such popular motifs of the age as wine-vase are used in ornamental niches along the whole mural surface. The same scheme of ornamentation has been followed on the main tomb.

The main plinth on which stands the tomb proper is of brick masonry and is 5'-4" in height and 266'-8" (81.28m) on each square side. The tomb proper is also a square building of 213'-4" (65.02m) side, being 21-4" (6.50m) in height. Each side has a bold frame containing the central arch, which projects forward a little, with five arches in each wing, there thus being 11 arches, of equal size, on each façade. Above them is only a cornice and at present, there is no Chhajja, an indispensable constituent of this design, to protect the arches. The parapet is made up of Jali railings and balustrades. On the whole, this is a simple composition and the tomb would have been passed over as an ordinary building had not a beautiful feature been introduced into it. It is the set of four minarets, each in five stages rising to a height of 85' (25.91m) which have been attached to the corners of the tomb. These are octagonal in plan, the main storey being of red sandstone. The upper three storeys and the crowning 'Chhatris' are of white marble. These storeys are separated by balconies and protected, originally, by Jali railings and balustrades. Above all, crowning the Minar, is an octagonal 'Chhatri', also of white marble with a similar balcony but with extremely slender pillars, octagonal Chhajja and a high cupola rising to half of the total height of the Chhatri. The emphasis, obviously, is on the verticality of the Minar. The main storey of the tomb, including the ground storeys of the Minars, is of red sandstone with which white marble has been lavishly used in inlaid mosaic. It is an intelligent system of panelling in slightly sunk niches. While façade dados bear geometrical designs, Guldastas and other typically Jahangiri motifs as wine-vase and dish-and-cup have been used on upper panels. Spandrels of the arches are of plain white marble, each bearing a circular inlaid medallion in low relief. The Minars bear chevron design, also in inlay technique. As a whole, each façade has been very simply, yet tastefully, decorated.

A broad arcaded Dalan runs round the tomb in the interior. It is divided into 11 vaulted bays, corresponding with the 11 arches, on either side. Vaults bear stalactite design in plain stucco. It is, obviously, a later restoration work and, in all probability, it was originally exquisitely painted in stylized, arabesque and floral designs. On it open a number of rooms which also originally painted. Probably, some figurative paintings were also done inside these rooms, the faint traces of which still exist.

The unique feature of this dalan is the glazed-tiled dados. Each has a stylized repetitive scroll on the border and a naturalistic plant motif in the centre. Turkish and peacock blues, greens and browns have been beautifully used on a yellow background, all in glazed-tiles. Lahore was, undoubtedly, during Jahangir's period, the home of glazed-tile work. But the exclusive use of this art on dados in such a predominantly stone building as this is an innovation in Mughal architecture. One could reasonably expect these dados to have been entirely painted or stone inlaid in polychrome, as it was being done contemporarily in other parts of the empire. Probably, the regional factor proved to be decisive in this case.

A broad passage from the central arch, on either side, leads into the central tomb-chamber. These four passages, providing approach to the tomb of Jahangir, have vaulted ceilings and are gorgeously painted and embellished. The tomb-chamber which is octagonal in plan being 26-6" (8.08m) in diameter, also has a vaulted ceiling. It has semi-octagonal alcoves on the corners. Passages are closed by Jali (screens) on N, E and S sides and the chamber is accessible only from the western dalan. The dados upto the apex of the arches are of white marble. Stucco work in stalactite design has been done above them, it was originally painted. In the centre is placed the tombstone of white marble, resting on a marble plinth which has beautifully moulded nook-shafts and floral compositions in inlay, in red and green. The tombstone also bears inlaid designs. On its sides are carved the 99 attributes of God and on the top extracts from the Holy Quran. At its foot is the Persian inscription:- "Marqad Munawwar Ala Hazrat Ghuphran-panah Nur'al-Din Muhammad Jahangir Badshah phi sanh 1037" (This is the illuminated resting place of His Majesty, the Asylum of Pardon, Nuruddin Muhammad Jahangir Badshah 1037/1627) recording the date of his death. The pavement has been similarly decorated with inlaid geometrical designs. All this has been ornately finished in white marble inlaid in polychrome in various designs. This ornamentation is exquisite.

Though the four "minars" which have spiral stairways are structurally attached to the corners of the main building, they are accessible only from the terrace and it is to it, rather than to the ground floor, that they are integrally associated. These minars, in fact, rise three storeys above the terrace and, though they form part of the design as a whole and without doubt the most important and predominant part of it, these minars are conceived in terms of and in relation to, the terrace and there is hardly any doubt that without them, the building would lose all its charm and effect and the terrace would look vacant and barren.

The tomb of Jahangir is perhaps the chief architectural pride of Lahore. If not the equal of Shah Jahan's Taj Mahal, it must rank with Humayun's Tomb at Dehli as one of the great relics of the best Mughal period. The mausoleum was completed by (Shah Jahan) in 1628.

It is approached through a great quadrangle occupying some 12 acres of ground, and it was here no doubt that those who came to visit the Emperor's tomb, would leave their equipages when they came on foot into the walled garden containing the tomb itself. It was once used as the engine yard and depot of the Railway, and proposals for its demolition actually received the sanction of the Government. It was rescued from base uses in about 1907, was put in proper order. It has on the west a large mosque, with three good domes.

The mausoleum itself lies in a walled garden of nearly sixty acres in extent, traversed by four bricked water channels. It stands on a raised plinth of red sandstone, some 275 feet square. Round the mausoleum runs an arcaded verandah, on which open a number of cells for readers of the Quran and other attendents. The tomb piece of the Emperor is within; on two sides are carved the ninety-nine attributes to God; on the top and foot are prayers to the deity; at the foot is recorded that this is" the illuminated resting place of His Majesty, the asylum of pardon, Nur-ud-Din Jahangir Badshah". The coloured inlay on the pedestal is of particular merit.

Two staircases lead up to a flat roof some 200 feet square; with a tessellated pavement at each corner, is a minaret four storeys high, inlaid with bands of variegated marbles and blocks of yellow stones, with marble cupolas on the top. These are some 85 feet in height from the plinth. In the centre of the roof is a low platform.

This low platform has given rise to a question of acute archaeological interest; was there at any date an upper dome over the roof of the tomb chamber? Tradition, though tradition is no very certain guide, is strong on the existence of a dome. The traveller Moorcroft, writing in 1820, says that the dome was believed to have been taken off by Aurangzeb "that his grandfather's tomb might be exposed to the weather". Alexander Burnes in 1831 and Von Orlich in 1843 attributed its removal to Bahadur Shah; in their case the motive assumed was merely a desire that "the rain and dew might fall on the tomb of the Emperor's ancestors". Later writers give other versions both of the date of the removal and its reason; the most interesting is the story that Ranjit Singh transferred the dome bodily to his baradari in the Hazuri Bagh. As to this, it is perhaps sufficient to say that there is good evidence of pilfering by Ranjit Singh from the tomb of Jahangir, but the story of the removal of the dome was not known till about 1880.

The building suffered much from the hands of one of the Bhangi triumvirate, Lehna Singh; and much of the trellis-work and marble was removed by Ranjit Singh for the temple at Amritsar. He gave the tomb as a residence to Mr. Amise, one of his French officers, who started to put it in order, but died soon after; it was subsequently occupied by an Afghan Sardar who did much to injure it by kindling fires in the halls and removing stones of value. It had been, as far as possible, restored by British Government.

There is a version that when the tomb was first built "a marble pavilion graced the central portion of the roof of the tomb, which would have added to its artistic appearance, but this has since disappeared." This was just a surmise. Jahangir's tomb belongs to a fully developed class of tombs which was in vogue during his age. This was an attempt to indianize an essentially exotic form of art and this tomb, as that of Noor Jahan, marks the culmination of the process which began with the building of Diwan-i-Khas at Fatehpur Sikri, built by Akbar between 1572 and 1585. This was now the stage that Mughal art had taken firm roots in the soil in less than half a century's time.

THE 'SERAE' OF JAHANGIR

The spacious serae of Jahangir is to the west of the mausoleum of the Emperor. It has two stately gateways, one to the north and the other to the south, both richly decorated with marble and red sandstone. To the west of the serae is a large mosque, with three splendid domes, supported by arches, the middle arch being lofty and decorated with flowers of marble stone beautifully set in red sand-stone. The gate to the east leads to the mausoleum of Jahangir.

The 'serae' was used as the manufacturing depot of the North Western Railway in British period. It is unquestionably a beautiful and spacious building, but badly misused by the local visitors and neglected by its Custodians. The visitors these days can hire taxis for return journey to the city just outside the main entrance of the complex.

THE TOMB OF NOOR JAHAN

Close to the mausoleum of Jahangir is the tomb of Noor Jahan (i.e. light of the world), the consort of Jahangir, whose life is equally romantic and eventful. She died on the 29th Shawal, 1055 A. H. (1638 A.D.), at the age of seventy-two, and was buried in the structure which she had herself caused to be erected. The marble sarcophagus was of most chaste workmanship, being of the same size and quality as those of Jahangir and Asif Jah at the same locality, with the names of God in their various signification engraved on it. It had, however, been removed. The vaulted rooms were all covered with marble and wrought with flowers of mosaic, but these were removed by Ranjit Singh. It is now a plain one storey building, with four main arches, and eight oblong openings in the centre, with three rows of arches beyond, the whole diameter being 135 feet. "The inner room has two tombs-one of Noor Jahan, and the other of Ladli Begam. Under this is a chamber inclosing the sepulchres. When Ranjit Singh stripped the building of its costly and precious ornamental stones, he had the barbarity to cause the subterranean room to be opened. What was discovered was two coffins suspended to iron swings. The swings were ruthlessly taken away, and the coffins buried under ground. The cell was left open to be desecrated by wild beasts."

The original name of the Noor Jahan, a heroine in the Moore's celebrated Lala Rukh;, was Mehr-un-Nisa (the sun of women). Jahangir called her Nur Mahal (light of the Harem), and she was also known by the name Noor Jahan (light of the world). She was the daughter of the Ghias Beg, son of Khwaja Muhammad Sharif, a noble of Teheran. Adverse circumstances compelled Ghias Beg, after the death of his father, to migrate with his two sons and one daughter to India. 'He was plundered on the way, and had only two mules left, upon which the members of the family alternately rode. On his arrival at Candahar, his wife gave birth to the celebrated Noor Jahan. In their destitution, the parents, despairing of being able to bring up the infant, exposed it on the roadside. Malik Masud, the leader of a caravan which happened to be travelling by the same route, saw the abandoned child; and full of compassion, and struck by its beauty, he took it up and employed its own mother as its nurse. He was known to Akbar, and through him Ghias Geg was introduced to His Majesty at the Court in Fatehpur Sikri. Noor Jahan's mother had free access to the Harem of the Emperor, and her daughter was her constant companion. As Noor Jahan grew up, her exquisite beauty, grace, and loveliness created a great sensation at Court. Prince Salem, aftwerwards Jahangir, then in the prime of his youth, was dazzled with her charms. The passion was mutual, but she had already been betrothed to a brave young Turkoman, named Ali Kuli Beg. The matter having reached the ear of Akbar, Nur Mahal was married to her betrothed and sent to Bengal. Jahangir had, however, .been scarcely a year on the throne when he commissioned his foster-brother, Qutb-ud-Din, to procure for him the object of his love. He went as viceroy to Bengal, and mooted the matter to Ali Kuli Beg, then known by the title or sobriquet of Sher Afgan, or the "lion queller," to whom Akbar had given a large estate in Burdwan. Sher Afgan deeply mortified at the haughtiness of the demand, drew his dagger, stabbed the viceroy to the heart, and was himself cut to pieces by the guards. Noor Jahan was sent to Agra, where she remained four years, in chaste seclusion, in the apartments of Sultana Ruqia Begam, daughter of Mirza Hindal. It was on a new year's day festival that, the Emperor happening to cast his eyes upon her, his passion for her was rekindled. She became the Queen of the East, and her influence was paramount. The Emperor writes of her: "Before I married her, I never knew what marriage really meant." Her fascinating beauty and her virtues went hand in hand with her talents and wisdom, and her lasting influence over the Emperor, and his counsellors was beneficial alike to the interests of the State, and the Court which she embellished by her taste. Her name was associated on the coin with that of the Emperor, in the graceful terms.'

"By order of the Emperor Jahangir the value of gold was increased a hundred fold by the name of the Empress Noor Jahan."

She was the Queen Regent, and, with the exception of the "Khutba" (prayer for the reigning monarch), she enjoyed all the privileges of royalty. Her father, who was made Prime Minister, received a flag and drum, which he was allowed to beat at Court, a rare privilege. Her eldest brother, Mirza Abu Talib, surnamed Shaista Khan, was made governor of Bengal, and as such, is often mentioned in the early history of the East India Company. Her other brother, Mirza Abdul Hasan Asif Jah, was raised to the command of 9,000. Her nurse, Dilaram, held the post of sadr of women (Sadr-un-nisa). She gave the tone to fashion, and possessed much taste in adorning apartments and arranging feasts. She had no children by Jahangir, and on his death and the capture of Shahryar, fifth son of the Emperor by his Hindu wife, to whom she had given her daughter (by Sher Afghan), Ladli Begam, in marriage, her influence ceased. Shah Jahan allowed her a pension of two Lacs of rupees per annum. She occasionally wrote Persian poetry, and like Salema Sultan Begam, second wife of Akbar, and Zebun-Nisa Begam, the accomplished daughter of Aurangzeb, wrote under the assumed name of Makhfi. She was the patron of orphan girls, and married not less than five hundred of such girls with her own funds. She devised many new female dresses, and designed new patterns of jewelry.

Mirza Ghias Beg, surnamed Itimad-ud-daula, died at Kangra, on his way to Kashmir, in 1622, and was buried in a fine mausoleum at Agra. The Mirza fell ill while Jahangir and Noor Jahan were on their way to Kashmir. The royal couple were recalled from a visit to Kangra fort, who arrived in time to find the Mirza dying. Pointing to her husband, the Emperor, Noor Jahan asked her father whether he recognized him. The dying man cited in answer the following verse of Anwari:-

"If one who is born blind stood here, He would recognise His Majesty from the brilliancy of his forehead." He died a few hours afterwards. Jahangir writes in the Tuzak that the Mirza Ghias Beg died of a broken heart, as he had lost his affectionate wife about three months back.

TOMB OF ASIF KHAN

Asif Khan's mausoleum lies to the west of the Serai of Jahangir, enclosed by walls of solid masonry. Asif Khan was the brother of Noor Jahan, and father of Arjmand Bano Begum or Mumtaz Mahal, the, favourite Queen of Shah Jahan. He died in 1633, leaving large property. His tomb was built by Shah Jahan, and historians speak not only of its costly inlay work but of the glory of its tiled decorations. The tomb was, like many others, rifled by Ranjit Singh, to build his baradari in the Hazuri Bagh.

Opposite the tomb of Jahangir, to the west, on a detached piece of ground, enclosed by high walls of solid masonry, is the tomb of Mirza Abul Hasan Asif Jah, the brother of Noor Jahan, and 'Wazir' of the Emperor. It is built in brick, in the form of an octagon, and supports a built dome of the same material. Asif Jah died on the 17th Shaban, 1051 A. H. or four years before his sister. According to Badshah Nama, it was built by Shah Jahan in four years, at a cost of three lacs of rupees. It was well-known for the beautiful glazed tiles which decorated its arched entrances; but of these decorations little is now left. The whole of the interior, with the floor, was covered with white marble, inlaid with costly stones, and the walls outside were embellished with a variety of stones, which were all removed by Ranjit Singh to decorate the temple at Amritsar, and used partly in other Sikh buildings. The edifice stands on a platform, the side walls of which were covered with the red limestone. At each of the four corners of this square was a reservoir of water, now, however, in ruins. The whole of this beautiful structure was in the midst of a spacious garden with fountains of water and beautiful walks, traces of which are still to be seen. Like the serae of Jahangir's mausoleum, the high and majestic gate of the tomb is towards the south. The mosque attached to it had been converted into a European residence during early British period.

The sarcophagus of the tomb is of pure marble, and the Arabic inscriptions on it are in the same style as those on the tomb of the Emperor Jahangir. It is not understandable that inspite of Government's order why these monuments are not being properly maintained and looked after and restored.

LAHORE FORT

With a galaxy of Muslim monuments Lahore richly deserve to be the custodian of proud architectural heritage. The main buildings of this period are found within the Fort. The Fort is the only place in Pakistan, which represents the different phases in the development of Mughal architecture. It, infact, possesses the work of four Mughal Emperors. The place gained prominence during the reign of Emperor Akbar, who demolished the old mud fort and constructed a new one of brick masonry. Later on, his successors Jahangir, Shah Jahan and Aurangzeb made numerous additions in the main building areas. The buildings of the time of Akbar and Jahangir are mainly of red sandstone with a preference given to the use of Hindu beams and brackets and decorative figures of animal like lion, elephant and peacock as well as sculptured gargoyle. The buildings of their successors, Shah Jahan and Aurangzeb – the Moti Masjid, the Naulakha pavilion and the Shah Burj, Shish Mahal are in a striking contrast with the former, with the use of white marble in place of sandstone and exuberance of the Persian motifs in the form of pietra dura work and mosaic of coloured stones.

The Ravi at one time ran clsoe under the northern wall of the Fort, "This river," said William Finch, 1611, "cometh from the East and runneth Westerly by the North side of the City; upon which within the Castle is the King's house passing in at the middle gate to the Riverward". The Ravi was so close to the town that Aurangzeb built a three mile embankment to protect it, and thereby altered the river's course; but pictures as late as 1854 show a small branch of the river still running near the Fort and cutting the Chauburji Minars.

Some form of fortress may well have been built on this site in early Hindu times; but, if so, no record or trace of it remains. The Lahore Hindu town was propbably near Ichhra or Mozang, and the small Hindu Mandir or shrine near the Hazuri Bagh, attributed to Loh, the titular founder of Lahore, seems to date back no further than the period of the Sikhs. The original of the Fort was no doubt erected by the viceroys of the Ghaznavid princes; the fort as we now see it was the work of Emperor Akbar, continued by Jahangir and completed by Shah Jahan. The only contribution of Aurangzeb was the Hazuri Bagh gateway, intended as an entrance to the forecourt of the Badshahi mosque. Designed and executed by different hands, it never possessed the unity of compostion which distinguishes the forts of Agra and Dehli. Neglected after the death of Aurangzeb and the transfer of the Court to Dehli, the Palace buildings had fallen into disrepair; it was left to the Sikhs and the British Military Works Department to convert neglect into ruin. Of the two, the Sikhs were the less flagrant vandals. They added some buildings and adapted others; but Ranjit Singh showed some respect for the State rooms of his Imperial predecessors; and if his ideas of art were barbaric, his intention here was clearly to embellish rather than to destory. The British Military Works, (occupation began in 1849), wrought havoc without scruple. Lord Curzon rescued the Moti Masjid and the small Khwabgah of Jahangir in 1903; but it was not until 1924 that the Fort, given up by the military authorities, came into the hands of the Archaeological Department to be saved for future.

To realize the general scheme of the buildings, the visitor had best proceed at once up the sloping ramp-a British innovation-and so arrive at the open space in the centre of the Fort. Standing there with his back to the City, he will be facing the Diwan-i-Aam or forty pillared hall of Shah Jahan; immediately behind this building is the quadrangle of Jahangir; to the left front is the Moti Masjid or Pearl Mosque, and behind that again the Shah Burj or Royal Tower are state rooms of Shah Jahan. The visitor is at the moment standing on the site of a great quadrangle, 730 by 460 feet, which faced the Diwan-i-Aam, and was enclosed on four sides by a range of vaulted chambers; of this cloister, probably built in Akbar's time, nothing now remains except the little court in front of the Moti Masjid. The cloister was shown on the Sikh map, and was demolished by the British.

We may now move to the Diwan-i-Aam, the Hall of Public Audience, erected by Shah Jahan, in the first year of his reign (1628), at the same time as a similar edifice in the Agra Fort. He ordered that a hall of forty pillars should be built in front of Jharoka or Balcony, on which the Emperor made his daily public appearance. The large platform on which the hall is raised was enclosed by a railing of red sandstones. All travellers who witnessed the daily court of the Great Mughal refer to these railings, which separated the different classes of nobles in attendance. Venetian Manucci, in his Storia do Mogor, describes at length a reception given here by Dara Shikoh, and Finch's narrative gives many details of the ceremony observed in 1611. Fra Sabastian Manrique describes the splendid Nauroz festival celebrated here in 1641. Ranjit Singh, though he used the Diwan-i-Aam, never seated himself on the Imperial throne, out of respect for the ancient rules. It is clear, however, from Honigberger's account that after the Maharaja's death his body lay here in state. After the British occupation the building was converted into a barrack; the outer archways were blocked up and the front enclosed. These structures have been removed, but the Diwan-i-Aam is now only a skeleton of the Imperial hall of Shah Jahan in the days of its splendour, when the descendant of Timur sat on the marble throne, and the halls adjoining the courtyard, hung with banners and tapestry, thronged with Amirs and Rajas in rich attire. It is fortunate that the Jharoka or State balcony is still in a fair state of preservation.

The Jharoka abuts from the back of a rectangular building of twelve small rooms, in which the painting on the roof apparently dates from Sikh times; it was here that Chet Singh was murdered in 1839 by Dhian Singh.

From the other side of this building one looks out on Jahangir's quadrangle. The buildings at the sides of the quadrangle still show the broad caves and heavily carved bracketing of Hindu origin which characterised Jahangir's architecture.

The only important existing monument of the time of Akbar is the Masjidi Gate. Built in 1566 A.D. as one of the entrances into the fort, its archway opens between two massively projecting bastions. In contrast can be seen a very well-laid area of the residential places, called Jahangir's Quadrangle. The quadrangle, which has suffered greatly from successive demolitions, once contained a palace garden, and Jahangir himself writes with rapture of this garden and the buildings which enclosed it. An inscription dated 1617 records the completion of the quadrangle by Mamur Khan, in the 12th year of the reign of Jahangir "the shadow of God, a Solomon in dignity, an Alexander in arms, the asylum of the Khilafate, the champion of the Faith." William Finch describes in detail the many mural pictures he saw in this building in 1611, including one of Christ and Virgin Mary. Leopold von Orlich, the German traveller, saw in 1843 a fete given in the garden of this court during the short reign of Sher Singh; the garden then contained a square marble reservoir with numerous fountains, in the centre of which stood a colossal silver peacock with outspread tail. This must have been removed in British times. At the further end of the quadrangle, towards the river front, was a building known as the 'Bari Khwabgah' or large sleeping place, to distinguish it from the small 'Khwabgah' of Shah Jahan.

Turning now to the left, or western side, we come to a second group of buiidings due to Shah Jahan. One of these is a small court containing a formal garden; on the marble platform in the centre there stood in Sikh times a pavilion (baradari) of gilt silver, which is said to have been sold by auction in 1849; the white marble on the path ways was taken by the Church at Mian Mir contonment. To the north or river front side of the garden was the Chhoti Khwabgah or sleeping room, probably one of the two buildings built by Shah Jahan in 1633, an open pavilion of white marble, the archways on the north side carrying pierced screens. The fountain basin in its interior was once inlaid with semi-precious stones. After 1849 the building was used by British as a church but was restored, at the instance of Lord Curzon.

Proceeding still by the left, one comes to a court, called in the Sikh times, the Khilat Khanah, which shows that at this period at leas it was used for the bestowing of robes of honour on distinguished nobles. On the south of this court were the royal baths, and on the south-west was the private mosque of the court ladies. There is also a later building erected by Rani Chand Kaur, who was here murdered at the instigation of Sher Singh.

Turn to the south, behind the royal baths, and visit the Moti Masjid or Pearl Mosque. There is no record to show by whom it was built, though its position at the north-west corner of Akbar's great quadrangle points that it might have been built by him. It was used as a Government Treasury both by Ranjit Singh and the British, its doorway was bricked up and vault dug beneath the marble floor. Close to this were the Makatab Khana building where the clerks sat to regester the visitors. There is a tablet on the front of this Building, which is termed partly of Jahangir's Quadrangle. It is written here that it was built by Abdul Karim Mamur Khan.

Returning now to the Khilat Khanah court, we pass on the left to a smaller court with a marble pavilion on the north-west dating from the reign of Ranjit Singh, and used by him as a court of justice. We have now reached the last court on the north-west, known by the name of Massamman Burj or octagonal tower. This name (abbreviated into Saman Burj), whence the guide books get what is a correct enough translation, dates only from Sikh times; when constructed by Shah Jahan the building was known as the Shah Burj.

Jahangir's Quadrangle on the back of Diwan-i-Khass was founded by Jahangir in 1617. The latter's fondness for nature is evident from the provision of a wide-open lawn with water fountains playing in the middle. The living rooms have a pillared frontage, each pillar, being facetted, shows a deeply carved chevron motif and supports a typical bracket of Akbari style – the bracket, which is directly derived from the older Hindu tradition, has a marvellous serpentine design with elephants riding on the top. Here one gets a glimpse of that style of architecture which Akbar followed. But it is in the reign of Shah Jahan that architecture achieved excellence. Shah Jahan's fondness for natives led him to go in for soft construction in white marble and create those architectural forms, which appealed to feminine beauty and grace. His Khwabgah (sleeping room), built in 1633, still preserve the marble doorframe and exceptionally beautiful marble screens.

The Diwan-i-Khas on the west of Jahangir's Quadrangle is an open arcaded pavilion wrought in the choicest marble. Its beauty is further doubled by the nicely cut marble screens on the west, the decorated parapet, and the ornamental floor well-laid with geometrical patterns together with a cup-shaped beautiful cistern inlaid with pietra dura work. Of this latter art the most beautiful example is the Naulakha. It was built in 1633 A.D. With its curvilinear roof this dainty little marble summer-house, renowned for its extremely minute and delicate pietra dura work wrought in precious stones, can easily boast of having the finest piece of inlay work. It is in the Shish Mahal which is now commonally so called. It was the Shah Burj, Royal Tower, or as Manucci transliterated it "the Xaxburg". An inscription over the Hathi Pol gate refers to the completion in 1631-32 of this Tower, which, as it says:-

> "for its immense height
> Is like the Divine Throne beyond imagination
> and conception.
> In purity, height, elegance and airiness, such
> a tower.
> Has never appeared from the castle of the sky,
> nor will.

Manucci in his travel account writes that the building in his time had "architectural adornment of curious enamel work with many precious stones. It is here that the King holds audience for selected persons, and from it views the elephant fights and diverts himself with them". The little building on the right was used by Ranjit Singh as a pay office, for his troops. On the north side of the square is the semi-octagonal Shish Mahal or palace of mirrors. The glass decoration dates from two periods; the ceiling is part of the original edifice, and is described by Abdul Hamid Lahori as made of "Aleppo Glass"; the inferior wall decoration dates from the Sikh period, as does also the wall painting. Part of the original decoration is seen in the pietra dura work in the spandrels over the arches, which has by miracle escaped the hand of the vandals. It was in the Shish Mahal that the treaty of Lahore was ratified by Lord Harding in 1846 and that in March 1849 the sovereignty of the Punjab was assumed by the British Government. In front of the Shish Mahal is an open marble court, a fountain playing in the middle. In the centre of the tank of fountain there is a platform made of marble where, now a days, on State visits instrumental music players sit and perform. A channel to an 'Abshar' (cascade) on the southern side connects this fountain. The cascade shows chevron design wrought in variegated marble of different colours so arranged that illusive ripples are caused when water flows over them. Next to the Shish Mahal on the west side, is an open pavilion known as the Naulakha, because it is said to have cost nine lacs of rupees; it is described by the court historians as "a pavilion of marble, with mosaics of cornelian, coral and other precious stones." On the whole. the buildings of the Shah Burj suffered less than others during the Sikh rule; it was the favourite residence of Ranjit Singh, which would perhaps account for the fountains on the top. Coming back to the court next to the Shish Mahal, the visitor will find a flight of steps leading downwards to the Hathi Pol or Elephant gate, which once formed a private entrance to the royal apartments. The Shish Mahal roof had been repaired by Punjab PWD in 1830s but it has again given way due to poor maintenance and misuse. It was coming down and has (now) been held by providing temporary supports on plank, foum and iron scaffolding. One would only prey and wish for its early restoration, as it is "the pride possession and a remarkable monument" not only in the fort but in the entire Pakistan.

Of the last phase of the Mughal period in the Fort is the Alamgiri Gate built by Emperor Aurangzeb in about 1673 A.D. It speaks of the great change that had come over the Mughal Empire in this sub-continent. It makes a great contrast with the Masjidi Gate of the time of Akbar. In its fluted towers rising above a lotus bud and having a kiosk as the crowing element, the Gate speaks of the softness and noble demeanor that came in with passage of time. The other most majestic monument is the Badshahi Mosque built opposite this gate in 1674 by Aurangazeb's foster brother and Master of Ordinance Fidai Khan Kuka. Conceived in a grand scale and constructed in chaste material the mosque calls to prayer by its tall minarets placed by an imposing gateway.

No description of the Fort will be complete without describing the pictured wall outside the Shah Burj Gate – the only specimen of figurative tile decoration and representation that survives from the Mughal period in Lahore. The decoration which was started during Jahangir's period in 1624 A.D. was completed in the reign of Shah Jahan in 1631. The pictures are decorated in mosaic and stand out boldly in gorgeous colours. They exhibit scenes of sports and daily life which enraptured the Mughal emperors. Here we can see elephant-fight, bullfight, camel-rise, Chaugan (Polo) and others in various moods and poses - a glimpse into the court life that the Mughals were keenly fond of, is found with ample depiction of the cultural life of the city. It is however unfortunate that this precious heritage is not being maintained and preserved and instead being misused. The fort is used for dinners etc. and film shooting. Above all, the fireworks are shortening the life of this precious heritage and needs to be avoided.

Outside the Fort there are a number of monuments of the Mughal period. These monuments evince much of the strength and solidity noted into Muslim architecture of the period, with exquisite decorative work at places like the tomb of Emperor Jahangir and Shalamar. In all these buildings there is in their spaciousness and setting something of the character of the nature-loving monarchs so fond of running water and lush green meadows and garden place. The masterly hand of these versatile builders "can be seen at these monuments where nature and man appear to have linked themselves so beautifully together".

THE BADSHAHI MASJID

To the west of the Lahore fort, is the Badshahi Masjid, or the Imperial mosque of Emperor Aurangzeb Alamgir. It is built on a raised platform, set on arches, and is considerably elevated above the level of the ground. The beautiful and stately gateway to the east, made of red sand-stone and marble, is approached by magnificent flight of large circular steps paved with a beautifully variegated stone from Kabul, known as Abri. These steps are twenty-two in number, the top one being 79 feet, 3 inches long, and the lowest more than 20 feet long. The gateway in its own right is a marvellous edifice. The mosque has been built, it is said in imitation of the mosque of Al Walid in Makkah. Above the arched entrance are many small turrets of red sand-stone and marble, and a tablet of white marble on the outer face of this entrance has the following inscription, in large letters, below the 'Kalima':-

"The mosque of the victorious and valiant king Muhy-ud-din Muhammad Alamgir. Constructed and completed under the superintendence of the humblest servant of the royal household, Fidai khan, Kuka, in 1084 A.H."

The inscription shows that the mosque was built in 1673 A. D., for Aurangzeb, by Fidai Khan, the foster-brother of the Emperor, mentioned by Bernier, as the great Moghal's Master of Ordnance. The mosque was built at a cost "exceeding six lacs of rupees."

The façade of the archway measures 66 feet, 10 inches long. The arched entrance opens on a large quadrangle, or court-yard, 530 feet long, N. and S., and 527 feet long, E. and W. In the centre is a reservoir of water for the ablution of the faithful. To the west of the square is the mosque itself, the roof of which is surmounted by three superb cupolas, or domes, of white marble, crowned with pinnacles, or spires, of brass, richly gilt and placed upon drum out of which they emerge in a curve, presenting an appearance resembling the form of a balloon. Under the domes of the mosque is the principal hall, with several arched entrances, facing the east; beyond this is another hall with arched entrances; the centre arch of red sand-stone, inlaid with ornamented white marble, is in the form of a massive gateway, and is wide and lofty.

Towards the western extremity, in the compartment beneath the central dome, is a handsome niche, or recess, looking towards Makkah (Khana-Kaaba). The spot here is expressly set apart for preaching and prayer, and on the pulpit close by was read by the high priest, on every Friday, the litany for the house of Timur. During the British period there were "offered, with a fervent heart, prayers for the long life of Her Most Gracious Imperial Majesty the Queen – Empress of India."

Each corner of the quadrangle has a minaret of red sand-stone, tall and majestic, towering above every other-object, and seen for many miles. Although simple in their design, and plain in their appearance, the towers stand conspicuous for their magnitude, solidity and size, and cannot fail to impress the observer with their colossal and solemn grandeur. The height of each minaret is 143 feet, 6 inches; its circumference outside 67, feet and inside 8½ feet. The minarets lost one storey, and were surmounted with cupolas which were dangerously shaken by an earthquake in 1840, and consequently had to be removed. Access to their summit is gained by a flight of narrow steps of red sand-stone in the interior, and from the top an interesting view of the surrounding country is obtained. Upon these towers Sher Singh, during his siege of the fort, in January 1841, posted his matchlock men, who, with their fiery weapons, spread destruction in the ranks of the besieged Dogras (in the palace), the supporters of Maharani Chand Kour, widow of the imbecile Kharak Singh. The bombardment resulted in the defeat of the Rani and the coronation of Sher Singh. When Hira Singh, on the murder of Sher Singh and Dhian Singh, besieged the Sindhianwalas, he placed 'Zamburahs', or light-guns, used in the mountain warfare of Kashmir, on the summit of the minars which overlook the fort. Hira Singh, as we know, triumphed and became Wazir in the place of his father.

The north and south of the quadrangle were overshadowed by rows of fine trees of the ficus Indica species, and lined with arcaded rooms, originally intended for the accommodation of the students studying at the mosque. Similar rooms existed along the eastern boundary of the edifice; but these were demolished by the British authorities.

The visitors and travellers describe (as in history books) the effect of the red sand-stone and white marble in the quadrangle of this superb and chaste mosque:- "The effect of the red sand-stone and white marble, relieved by nothing but green trees within the square was very simple, and very impressive."

It is related that the materials of this mosque were originally collected by Prince Dara Shikoh for the construction of a spacious mausoleum over the remains of Hazrat Mian Mir, his spiritual guide; but, before he could accomplish his design, he met his death at the hands of his crafty brother, Aurangzeb who, on ascending the throne, confiscated the materials, and used them in building of the mosque bearing his name.

The Mosque was used as a 'stable' and 'magazine,' for keeping military stores, during Sikh period. Some of the rooms on the side of courtyard adjoining fort were also used as wine factory by the Sikhs. According to Kanahaya Lal lot of precious stone slabs were removed during the Sikh period from the Mosque.

During Sher Singh's attack on the fort and bombardment by forces of Maharani Chand Kor the greatest damage was done to the Mosque. It was practically deserted place, only under the use of Sikh military. After annexation of Punjab in 1849 the British also used the entire Mosque area as a barrack for the British forces. Modifications in the side rooms were also made but finally when they settled down, on the representations from the Muslims, the Mosque was restored to the community in 1856 but it was in no way worth use for prayers as a religious place. Some Muslims led by one Khan Bahadur Barkat Ali Khan raised contributions and arranged for the working of water supply (well) and motivated the Muslim community to use the place for prayers etc. A Committee was set up to look after the same but lot of work required to be done for which no funds were available. Notable Muslims under the guidance of Cap. Nisbet, Deputy Commissioner, Lahore, managed for more contributions with which minor repairs were completed. It was latter in the early 20th century that finally a cess was levied on Muslim landowners throughout Punjab with which fallen minarts of the Mosque were completed and the entire courtyard done up in red sand stone with proper water supply arrangements. Since then the Mosque is regularly in use for prayers with an 'Imam' paid by Government. The Prime Minister, Chief Minister and Governor come to the Mosque for Eid congregations and other religious occasions. This imposing religious monument by Aurangzeb Alamgir is obviously the identity of this historic and noble city. The management of the mosque now vests in the Auqaf Department. This from hundred year old monument require maintenance and care. Unfortunately it is not getting due attention.

THE MOSQUE OF MARIAM ZAMANI

This is one of the most ancient mosques of the city. It is situated close to the Masti (Masjidi) Gate of the city, opposite the eastern walls of the fort. As the inscription on the northern gateway shows, it was built in 1023 A.H. (1614 A.D.), during the reign of Jahangir, by his mother, Mariam Zamani. According to the Ain-i-Akbari, she was the daughter of Raja Behari Mal, and sister of Raja Bhagwan Das. The style of the building is transitional between the Pathan and Mughal. Its massive domes, one large and two side one, and bulky arches, are in the old Pathn style, but the gateways, the balconies and the side-rooms are more Mughal in their construction than Pathan. The mosque is surmounted with four arched towers, one at each corner. It is built of bricks, cemented by chunam of the best quality, so excellent, indeed, that the strength of the building seems to depend entirely on its adhesive properties. In the centre of the courtyard of the mosque is a fountain of water for the ablutions of the faithful. The Masjid was used by Ranjit Singh as a gun and powder factory, and on that account came to be called the "Barud-Khana Wali Masjid". The establishment was under the superintendence of Jawahar Mal, Mistri. The mosque was restored to the Muslims during British period by Major McGregor, Deputy Commissioner of Lahore, in 1850, together with the shops and houses attached to it. It was repaired from subscriptions raised by the Muslims. The Archaeology Department looks after the mosque which is a protected monument.

Inscription on the northern gateway:-
"God is great." "God be thanked through whose grace
"Under the auspices of His Majesty this building was completed.
"The founder of the edifice, the place of salvation, is the Queen Mariam Zamani." On the central arch is inscribed the Ayat-ul-Kursi.

The mosque covers an area of land measuring 135 feet 6 inches by 127 feet 6 inches. It is constructed of brick masonry and rendered with plaster, and is a massive structure representing a transitional phase of architecture between the Lodhi and the Mughal periods. It has two entrances through deeply recessed arched-gateways on its north and east sides. A flight of four steps in each gateway leads downward to the main courtyard, measuring 123 feet by 83 feet. The courtyard was originally enclosed by rows of cells on its north and south, some portion of which still exists. On the east, along the gate, is a 17 feet wide platform on which stands an enclosure consisting of an octagonal domed tomb and some other modern graves.

In the centre of the courtyard a tank for ablution, measuring 31 feet 5 inches by 26 feet 3 inches, has been erected probably at a later date. A modern roof of reinforced cement concrete (R.C.C.) supported by two rows of round pillars, covers the tank partially on its four sides. The courtyard must have been paved with brick tiles in usual Mughal fashion, but it has now been completely re-laid in modern bricks. At the north-west and the south-west corners, beside the prayer chamber, are located the old stair-cases leading to the roof. Similarly, on the north-eastern and south-eastern corners were stair-cases leading to the roof of the cells. Only their traces are left now.

The prayer chamber of the mosque, however, is of special interest Architecturally, it is an oblong structure measuring internally 130 feet 6 inches from south to north 34 feet from east to west. It has five compartments divided by heavy engaged arches supported by massive jambs and surmounted by high domes. The central dome is the highest, placed on a high and round neck (11 feet 1 inch). The double door consists of two shells-outer (3 feet 6 inches thick) and inner which is of stucco. A wooden framing connects the two shells for re-enforcement. The outer shell has a small arched opening on the west.

The front openings of the chambers, five in number, possess for centred arches, the central one being the highest and the biggest with a high parapet and a projected frame. The whole outer surface of the front has been treated with thick lime plaster creating decorative arched-panels in recess. Inside the prayer chamber, there is a series of high and deep arched-recesses set in all the five compartments on the west. The central niche, the mehrab, has an engrailed arch, treated specially with profuse stucco ornamentation, both geometric, floral and inscriptional. The half-domed niche of the central arched-opening and the mehrab has been filled with low stallactites. The remaining four compartments have the same engrailed-arch treatment, though comparatively smaller and less decorative.

At the four corners of the prayer chamber are placed small square-shaped pavilions (6 feet 10 inches) with four arched-openings surmounted with cupolas placed on octagonal drums. Originally, the cupolas were crowned with low crestings and finals like the five bigger domes over the main prayer chamber. These have now considerably decayed. A visit to the mosque educates one in early Mughal architecture at Lahore.

THE CHAUBURJI

The building known as Chauburji, on the Multan road, is the old gateway of the garden of Zeb-un-Nisa, or Zebinda Begam, the learned daughter of Aurangzeb, whose poetical name was Makhfi. The outer side of Minars are enamelled and decorated with blue and green encaustic tiles and frescoes of exquisite beauty, which, notwithstanding the lapse of about four centuries are as fresh and brilliant as ever. The garden originally extended from Nawan Kot to the city of Lahore on the west, but not a vestige of it now remains. The uppermost part of the building has the Ayat-ul-kursi, a 'Surah' from the Holy Quran, inscribed on it in Arabic letters of blue colour, worked in porcelain. At the end of it the year of foundation of the building is given, namely, 1056 A. H. (1646 A. D.) in the year following which Aurangzeb was sent on an expedition to Balkh, but was compelled to retreat. Above the arch are inscribed the following verses in Persian:

"This garden, in the pattern of the garden of paradise, has been founded, (The second line has been effaced)"
"The garden has been bestowed on Mian Bai."
"By the bounty of Zebinda Begam, the lady of the age."

Three towers of this picturesque building survived the wreck of time, but the fourth, to the north-west, with a portion of the wall on that side, had fallen down. On either side of the arches north and south of the middle arch, is inscribed the word "God," in blue Arabic letters, enclosed by a circle. There had been a dome, but it has disappeared.

Mian Bai was a favourite female attendant of Zebinda Begam, and when the garden was complete, the royal lady bestowed it on her. According to Shah Jahan-nama, the gift of the garden was made to Mian Bai under the orders of Zebinda Begam, her attendant, Mian Bai, having supervised the construction. One day, as the garden was approaching completion, the Princess was on her way to it when she heard the people saying that the royal lady was going to see Mian Bai's garden. Seeing that the garden was already known after the name of her slave girl, she resolved to make her a present of it. As she reached the garden and stepped into the gateway, Mian Bai came forward to receive her, made her obeisance, welcomed her and prayed for her long life. The prayer was a sign for the gift of the garden, and the Princess, as she had indeed already resolved, forthwith made a gift of it to Mian Bai. The fact of the gift is recorded in the Persian verses on the gateway. After this, the Princess commenced laying out her own garden on the site of the Nawan Kot, which, after her name, came to be called the garden of Zebinda Begam.

On the same road to the extreme north south of the Civil station happened to be spacious house built by Lord Lawrence in 1849. It became subsequently the property of Charles Boulnois, Esq., first Barrister Judge of the Chief Court of the Punjab who made large additions to it, and then of Sir Meredith Plowden, Chief Judge of the same Court. This is where the Director of Industries office is located (Poonch House).

When British occupied Punjab it had only these pillars left as the river was just flowing underneath the monument. Later it was converted into a storm drain. The monument was surrounded by squatters and it was only under specific orders of Prime Minister Nawaz Sharif that the surroundings were cleared by then the Director General L.D.A Mr. Hafizullah Ishaque under his day and night personal supervision and the place made worth visit. The Archeology Department had also rebuilt the lost pillar a couple of years back. The Chauburji monument is now in the centre of a round about where the lower Mall, Fateh Sher road and Lahore road meet and join the old Multan Road. Small iron fence has been provided around the edifice.

THE NILA GUMBAD

The Nila Gumbaz (Gumbad), or the blue tower, is a lofty and spacious dome surmounted by a cupola of porcelain. It is situated opposite old Ewing Hall and King Edward Medical College. Beneath the roof of the vault are enshrined the remains of a Ghaznivide saint, named Abdul Razzak Makki, of Sabzwar, who, coming from Ghazni, settled in Lahore, in the time of Humayun. The mausoleum was erected in his memory by his disciples, who also constructed a large mosque attached to it. During the Sikh period the Masjid was used as artillery quarters, and in the commencement of the British period as a Mess for the army unit in Anarkali cantonment. But it was restored to the Muslims in 1856, and has been kept in good repair by the Muslim merchants of Anarkali, though the mausoleum itself has been very much neglected. The dome is said to be situated in the serae of the (late) Sheikh Rahim Bakhsh.

The saint, according to his will, was burried in the closet in which he was accustomed to say his prayers.

The Masjid attached with tomb is large and commodious, and provided with a spacious court-yard and a large reservoir for the ablution of the devotees. A Madrassa for teaching the holy Quran is also attached to it.

It is now surrounded by shops on the front by a Cycle market. Just touching berm of road a big water reservoir with fountains has been built. This was constructed on orders of late General Ghulam Jilani Khan the Governor of Punjab in this Chowk when century celebration of King Edward Medical College were being undertaken. Across the fountains is the old F.C College's building. From the chowk moving north one enters the famous Anarkali Bazar and westerned on the Mall.

THE LAHORE MUSEUM

Opposite the university hall (old campus) on the Mall stands a most imposing building which houses the relics of Pakistani History and culture. This is Lahore Central Museum, which has built up its collection over a period of about 150 years. The visitor to Lahore is advised not to miss a visit to the place which is really rewarding.

Where and at what premises the Museum was set up for the Ist time? It is learnt that it made its beggings somewhere in the Baradari of Wazir Khan, where afterwards the Anarkali Book Club was located. The working of the Lahore Central Museum is also confirmed from the Notification issued on October 2,1858 regarding a meeting at the Museum Premises, which was spacious and commoditious enough to cater to the requirements of other departments. These arrangements appear to have continued for quite sometime.

LONDON EXHIBITION 1864

In the year 1861, the Punjab Government set up District Committees headed by the Deputy Commissioners which were given the task of collecting products of Punjab which were to be sent to London for an exhibition being arranged there. Mr. T. H. Thoronton in his instructions to the Deputy Commissioners specified their duties to take immediate measures for making known the objects of the exhibition, its conditions, making rough selections and transmission of articles. The collection of articles was to be contributory and inducing the public. Guidelines were also furnished about the nature of articles; "Raw Products" were to be preferred, with reference to items of commercial value excluding common bids of raw produce. With regard to Art and Manufactures which promoted material for the future Museum, items were to be of quality which could compete with those of other parts of India "Good specimens of Shawl weaving "Koft Gari" of Gujrati work, gold and silver brocade, Lacquered pottery, wood emamelling; Papier Macheivory work, silk, velvet and fine cotton fabrics were considered acceptable.

It is recorded that Museums were established prior to this as District Museums and maintained at Dehli, Lahore, Multan, Amritsar and Sialkot. The Central Lahore Museum, with its Curator was there since 1858, as an independent institution and entity. The exhibition place for London show was developed as a separate project for the event exclusively, although motive at initial stages was knowledge and exploitation of resources.

When the exhibition closed in April, 1864, the whole building was of course occupied for a considerable time by the left over of the collection; and after all was cleared, the building (later known as Tolinton Market) remained empty (partly) for sometime. In October, 1864 on the occasion of the great Durbar, it was used as the place of distribution for "Khilluts". Subsequently the building was (one half) re-roofed and re-floored with pucca bricks and then divided into two parts by a beautiful double screen of glass and carved wood which being double, formed passage across the centre from door to door; access being gained to either part of building by doors on the screen itself.

When these arrangements were complete, the remains of old Museum collection were removed into the end of the building farther from the bazar Anarkli side, while the other end was left vacant. Several public entertainments were held in here too. Subsequently the other half was also re-roofed and with a view to protect from dust, the screens already alluded to, were raised to the roof, by a construction of Gothic frame-work and glass to match the original screen below. This, done, it was found that the requirements of the Museum were greater than the one-half of the building could provide, for, and consequently the other half was taken up also. The original division was maintained to contain the raw produce and Natural History together within an annexe containing antiquities. The newly acquired half was devoted to manufactured products, fine Arts, ethnographic specimens and the collection of coins.

Once fixed in the building the collection began rapidly to increase. Besides the remains of the old Museum that existed since 1858 in the building occupied by the Anarkali Book Club, a considerable addition resulted from the Exhibition of 1864. Nearly all the raw produce that survived the exhibition during several months, a number of models, and a number of manufactured specimens, were taken over for the museum.

The subsequent growth of the collection had been the result of some purchases, but principally of the contribution of various districts pursuant to instructions issued by the Government. Quarterly lists of the contributions were notified in the Gazette but the more important acquisitions in various departments and noteworthy were the antiquities, natural history and ethnography.

An interesting addition was relic of Greek art i.e. the base of the Greek columns of the Ionic order which was discovered by General. A. Cunningham near Sehah-ki-dera in the Rawalpindi district. This place is supposed to be the site of the ancient Taxila. Major Hall contributed to the Museum a large stone figure of Buddha and also a beautifully sculptured figure from the ancient Taxila.In the Ethnographic Department the museum was helped by Dr. Cayler and Dr. Leitner.Dr. Cayler contributed a number of specimens illustrating the products of Ladakh, and later complete collection of dresses, manufactures and agricultural products of these countries. Dr Leitner donated collection of dresses and other curiosities that he brought from Little Tibet and the Daro country. These included some interesting Tibetan manuscripts, and a number of other specimens. A place had been proposed for a complete ethnographic gallery of dresses, exhibition of the costumes of the various tribes in the hills and plains of the Punjab.

The building had been also beautified by presentation of two marble statues and some other specimens of marble vases. The total number of contributions to the collection upto 31st March 1868 was over hundred specimens. The Museum was very favourably situated and became a place of attraction for visitors.

While the various Local Museums in the Punjab were designed primarily to illustrate the products, trade, industry and Arts of the Districts in which they were situated, the Central Museum at Lahore was designed to represent the products and manufactures of the whole Province, and with this object it was divided into four departments: Raw products, Manufactured articles, Antiquities, Coins, and Natural History.

A Committee for cooperation was set up in each District, to correspond with the Central Committee at Lahore; that if any objects of interest or curiousity was to be reported. The small expenditure required for this purpose was to be met from local bodies funds; and for expenses of carriage to Lahore, or for the purchase of manufactured articles or other valuables which it may be desirable to obtain, the Curator of the Central museum was to arrange funds. Since the exhibition place was a temporary structure, it was again specially done up and preparations made for housing and now locating the Lahore Central Museum in that place for which the instructions in question were issued by Government.

The Museum remained in the exhibition building for a long period. In March 1872 a Committee, was set up known as Mayo Memorial Committee to establish a suitable Memorial in honour of the Late Viceroy. The Committee accomplished its objective by raising contributions and free will offerings and collected Rs.66,053/-. Regarding the use of the funds; further a special Committee was set up which recommended that half the amount be used for a School of Arts and half to replace the condemned building of Museum of which Rai Kanyha Lal even submitted a design. This was conveyed by Mr. Brandrath, the Commissioner of Lahore, to the Provincial Government. The Committee also recommended that the Government might join the Museum to the School of Arts. The newly appointed Principal, Lahore School of Arts in his letter dated 27 May 1875 advised that from the Art Teacher's point of view the connection of the School of Arts with the Museum is most desirable as the present building was not weatherproof and unsuitable for Museum in the summer months, the valuable collection was likely to suffer both from heat and wet and new museum building was an emergent necessity. It was also felt that Museum should follow the commencement of the Arts School. The names of Mr. Purdon and Major Mant were suggested for design. Lengthy correspondence and discussions continued about location, funding, design and other connected matters and finally after 30 years temporary abode in "Ajaib Ghar" the Present building was decided to be constructed in 1887 as a result of public subscriptions to commemorate the Jubilee of Her Majesty Queen Victoria. The foundation stone was laid in 1890 by His Royal Highness Prince Victor, the Prince of Wales. Mr. Lockwood Kipling was then Curator of Central Museum Lahore. The design of the building was prepared by Sardar Sahib Ram Singh. The building was completed in 1893, and all the collections were immediately transferred to it.

Because of Kipling's association with Art, and Art school as also syallabus the Museum was mainly taken advantage of by the students of the Mayo School of Arts, who used the exhibits in the museum under the supervision of their teachers for the purpose of getting ideas for new designs. Some other colleges also used to send their students under charge of their teachers to study the collections chiefly in the Geology, Natural History and Sculptures Section. Lectures and Study shows were also held. Additions and acquisitions was a continued process. The Treasure Trove Act helped a lot in adding to the collection of coins. Purchases were also effected in respect of Art and manufactured items included Paintings and drawings. Punjab hill painting series were acquisitions of the late twenties. All the galleries were open to public except the new gallery which was mostly used by the Principal, Mayo School of Arts for his exhibitions of craft work.

The Lahore Museum continued to grow and gained much from the archaeological excavations and remains in the country but these were mostly industrial products, artifects, statutes and archaeological fragments without any systematic arrangement. Inspite of this it was the most precious and valuable asset for cultural history of the area. In 1947 the collection was divided between India and Pakistan, which gaps will take long to complete. The condition of Museum and its maintenance deteriorated and gradually after partition, until the Punjab Government came to its rescue in late 1950s. The building at that time was in a bad shape with broken floors leaking roofs and no electricity. The institution was without laboratory, workshop and other public utilities etc.

The Museum was closed for quite sometime for reorganisation and rehabilitation. Extensive repairs were carried out both to the building and the wood-works. Additional construction took place. A Carpentry, a laboratory and studio emerged along with canteen, parking and a shop. Separate sections were organized for study of manuscripts, paintings and cataloguing work accelerated. The compound of the Museum was done up in consultation with horticulturists and a properly landscaped lawn developed. Of course, additions continued to be made, staffing position multiplied against the pre-partition nucleus arrangement. During this re-organization and re-doing the industrial exhibits/ material were transferred to the Industries Department leaving the Museum only with cultural and historical assets. The pattern of acquisitions of antiquities has too, undergone a change. While in the pre-partition days the field offices used to help collect antiquities for the institution now acquisitions through purchases is the only mode for which, of course, the funds are limited and Government's priorities otherwise. Inspite of these constraints the institution has reasonably added to its collection of antiquities, manuscripts, documents and books both through public, generous donations and purchases. Presently as the Museum exists it can be divided into 7 Sections: i.e. Historical collection, 2. Ancient Hindu Section, 3. Buddhists sculpture, 4. Islamic, 5, Muslim relax, 6. Paintings, coins and 7. Pakistan movement Section. In 1965 again some steps were taken towards the renovation of Lahore Museum by Mr. B. A. Kureshi, the then Chief Secretary and later Chairman of Museum's Board of Governors. The Museum was re-organized and new additions made. For example, the historical Jain Temple and ethnological I and II Galleries were added in late 1960s. The Pakistan Postage Stamps Gallery was set up. Other additions include manuscripts, calligraphic illustrations, of Arts and crafts, and Coins and medals section.

The Museum has invaluable historical collection on cultural history of Pakistan from the earliest to the present times. Some objects have come from other parts of the world. The objects from the sites of Harrappa and Mohenjodaro, displayed in the gallery, unfold the world's earliest town planning. The undeciphered script of seals stands to be a mystery for archaeological scholars. As a whole all these finds represent Paleolithic, microlithic and Neolithic periods of Pakistan's history.

Buddhist Sculpture collection in the Museum is unique. It is evidence of a wonderful civilization which once flourished in Gandhara region. The sculpture of fasting Sidhartha of second century is notable for its artistic accomplishment. It manifests the Greek and Roman influence in the region. The sculpture depicting the miracle of Sarawati is a master piece, as it has been carved out from sixty-eight figures in motion into one stone mass. It belongs to the second century. The sculptures displayed in the gallery present complete sequence of the story of Buddha from his birth to death. The Buddhist specimens also include pieces of Kushan at Mathura. Statutes, reliefs and architectural fragments represent Jainism.

The Islamic collection of the Museum manifest cultural history of Muslims in the fields of Miniature paintings, manuscripts, calligraphy, architecture and various kinds of crafts including wood work, papiermache, arms, carpets, shawls, textiles, ceramics, jewellery and remarkable and rare items as the large sized carpet of the Mughal period, a Safvid Sword, the famous astrolabes produced at Lahore. Humayun's wood-carved Quranic verses of Ayatual Kursi, and Wooden door of Akbar's time.

The recently established manuscript section contains a large number of manuscripts of the Holy Quran in Arabic, Persian, Urdu, Punjabi, Pashtu, Turkish, Sindhi, and other languages, transcribed in various styles of writing on palm leaves, hide, paper, rugs, cotton and other materials. The Kufic Quran is a unique specimen of the Seljuqi period. There are many other pride items in the collection, some of which are Herati Quranic manuscript of Shahrukh's time; the Quran transcribed for Egypt's Mamluk Ruler Abu Saeed Jaqamaq; Khannsh-e-Niazmi from the library of Jalal-ud-Din Khan of Azerbaijan; illustrated Shah Nama of the time of Shah Suleman (1667-94), oldest manuscripts of Devan-e-Talib-Aml, Royal manuscript of Sahih Bukhari from the Library of Shah Jahan and Aurangzeb Alamgir, Devan-e-Hafiz inscribed by Abdul Rashid Delmi, text of Tafsir by Abul Faizi.

The Museum has a rich collection of miniature paintings. The earliest examples are from the manuscripts of Kalpasutras, the Jain religious text from Gupt (India) of the fifteenth century. The Mughal paintings display Persian influence and subsequent developments under the Mughals themselves. The productions of their own type in the world. Modern painting collections include specimens of almost all modern painters of Pakistan like Abdur Rehman Chughtai, Ustad Allah Bakhsh, Zain-ul-Abidin, and Anna Molka which owe their existence due to the donations made by Faqir Jalal-ud-Din Trust, Maulana Hifzur Rehman, Khawaja Abdur Rahsid Kamil and many others in addition to purchases.

The Museum includes the earliest issues of coins, known as Punch Marked, produced in the fourth century B. C. and subsequent periods. It also contains the first Muslim coins issued by Mahmood Ghaznvi in Lahore, bearing the inscription of Mahmoodpur, the then name of Lahore. The collections are housed in lockers and scholars can see on request. However, for instructional purpose, the Gallery of Coins and Medals has been recently organized with a display of replicas of the originals.

The Museum in its present condition, according to the management presents panorama of history of Pakistan and culture from the earliest of modern times. The most significant latest addition to the Museum is the establishment of freedom gallery, which contains pictorial scenes of the struggle of Muslims in the Sub-continent. This is significant but slightly different aspect of the museum in cultural and historical assets.

ZAMZAMAH

As one travels east (from Post Master General Office) up the Mall today, one by one the British period structures reveal themselves; the Punjab University (old campus); the Town Hall, the Museum; Kim's gun, (Zamzamah); the High Court; the Cathedral; and the General Post Office.

Facing College of Arts opposite Punjab University (old campus) on a raised platform near the entrance to the Lahore Museum, is the Zamzamah, famous as Kim's gun placed in the entre of the Mall Road. It was placed here on the occasion of the visit of His Royal Highness the Duke of Edinburgh to Lahore in 1870, and Rudyard Kipling wrote of it, 'Whoever holds Zamzamah the fire breathing dragon, holds the Punjab, for the great green bronze piece is always first of the conqueror's loot. This ancient piece was one of two identical guns cast at Lahore, in 1757, under the direction of Shah Wali Khan, Prime Minister of the Abdali King Ahmad Shah Durrani. A mixture of copper and brass, it is said to be composed of metal vessels taken from each house in Lahore tax, which were then melted down and cast. Ahmad Shah used it in the famous battle of Panipat in 1761; afterwards, on his way to Kabul, he left it with his governor Khwaja Ubaid. He took the other gun, but lost it while crossing the Chenab River.

In 1762, Hari Singh Bhangi attacked the village of Kot Khwaja Said two miles from Lahore. This village housed the arsenal of the Mughal governor, and Hari Singh Bhangi succeeded in seizing all the artillery, guns, ammunition, including the prized Zamzamah, henceforth known as the "Bhangi Top". It lay unmounted in the Shah Burj at Lahore until 1746, when it was retaken by two Bhangi Sardars, who were Sikh warriors. Two days later, Chait Singh Sukerchakia came to Lahore to demand his share of the spoils. The Bhangi Sardars were unwilling to part with any part of their recently conquered territory, and sought to pay him off by offering him the Zamzamah with the 'topes' that its unwieldy weight would prevent him from carrying it away. But the Sukerchakia chief called all his men together and carried it off to his fort in Gujranwalla. It was subsequently captured by other rival clans and moved from camp to camp, eventually arriving in the Bhangi Fort at Amritsar, where it remained until 1802. Ultimately, however, Ranjit Singh took possession of it, and expelled the Bhangis from Amristar.

This famous gun came to be regarded as a talisman for supremacy, and Ranjit Singh used the Zamzamah in his campaigns in Daska, Kasur, Sujanpur,

Wazirabad and Multan. But after being seriously damaged in the last battle, it was removed in 1818 to Lahore and displayed outside the Dehli Gate of the old city. From there it eventually made its way to the front of the Lahore Museum, a proud but benign trophy from the Sikhs, through the British Raj and Independence, to the present day.

The gun had been repaired a couple of years back as the wooden part had been damaged due to weathering effect. This was replaced, the Gun War, polished (with anti rust material) and a proper stand erected and again placed near a water tank prepared by the pedestal. Zamzamah is one of the Lahore symbols.

THE TOMB OF ANARKALI

Anarkali (the pomegranate blossom), was the title given to Nadira Begum, or Sharf-un-Nisa, one of the slaves of the harem of the Emperor Akbar. One day, while the Emperor was seated in an apartment lined with looking glasses, with the youthful Anarkali attending him, he saw from her reflection in the mirror that she returned Prince Salem (afterwards Jahangir) a smile. Suspecting her of suggestive insinuation with his son, the Emperor ordered her to be buried alive. She was accordingly placed in an upright position at the appointed place, and was built round with bricks. Salem felt intense remorse at her death, and, on assuming sovereign authority, had an immense superstructure raised over her sepulchre. The sarcophagus is made of a block of pure marble of extraordinary beauty and exquisite workmanship. It is, according to Mr. Eastwick, "one of the finest pieces of carving in the world." On the top are inscribed the 99 attributes of God, and on the sides is engraved the following Persian couplet, composed by Jahangir, her royal paramour:-

"Ah! Could I behold the face of my beloved once more, I would give thanks unto my God until the day of resurrection."

On the north side of the sarcophagus, below the ninety-nine attributes of the Deity, is the inscription:-

"The profundly enamoured Salem, son of Akbar," Salem being the name of Jahangir when a Prince.

The inscription shows how passionately fond Salem had been of Anarkali, and how deeply her death had grieved him. It is the spontaneous outcome of a melancholic mind, the irrepressible out-burst of an affectionate heart. The building was used as the Protestant Church, and known as St. James's Church, Anarkali. When it was about to be utilized as a Church, it is said the body was exhumed and buried under one of its turrets. The marble sarcophagus, which covered it beneath the central dome, was at the same time removed, and kept in a side chamber. The date given in letters and in figures is 1008 A. H. (1599 A.D), which refers to the death of Anarkali. On the west side of the sarcophagus above the words "In Lahore," is another, date 1024, A. H. (1615 A.D.), which is the date of the building of the tomb. Akbar died on the 13th October 1605, and thus the building was completed ten years after his death.

The building is octagonal in shape and roofed with a vast and lofty dome, supported inside by eight massive arches, 12 feet, 3 inches thick. It is a masterpiece of solid masonry work of early Mughal period, and is neatly and prettily fitted up. It measures 75 feet, 6 inches from E. to W.

In the time of the Mughal Emperors, extensive gardens surrounded this imposing mausoleum, and several beautiful buildings were attached to it, but not a vestige of them now remains. The Ravi then flowed under its walls. In the time of Maharaja Ranjit Singh it was occupied by Kharak Singh, the heir-apparent, but was subsequently given to M. Ventura, the Italian officer of the Sikh Government, who converted it into a private residence. Adjacent to it was the grand house of M. Allard, and in front of it, a parade ground intervening, were the lines of the Sikh regiments and battalions under the orders of the French officers previously named.

When the Punjab was annexed by the British Government the tomb, which happened to be close to Residency office, was used for sometime as clerical office. When Board of Administration was shifted from Residency building, on 15th March 1851 it was used as church.

Dr. Ahmad Nabi a known historian and Archaeologist analyses the story as a whole in its socio-historical perspective. It has been said elsewhere that the story came down to us through William Finch who heard it while passing through Lahore. It is noteworthy to see that he reached Lahore on 4 February 1611, and left the place on 18th August the same year. It means that the total period of this Englishman's stay at the 'Dar ul Sultanat' was not more than six months. During this period, he was passing through an anxious time due to his difficulties with his master at Akbarabad (Agra) and more so because of his own tactless handling of a business deal. It was hardly possible for him to get himself familiar with the traits of the local society, nor could he care to verify the street gossip which he simply recorded as an anecdote in his Journal which he was maintaining as a daily diary.

It is, however, noteworthy that no mention of it has been found in the contemporary, near-contemporary or later historical literature. It may plausibly be argued that the contemporary as well as later court chroniclers would have hardly dared to write about such happenings in the royal harem to defame their royal patrons. However, there were still some impartial historians and authors like Mulla Abd-ul-Qadir Badauni, Khafi Khan and others who were really critical historians. Bada'uni, for instance, never spared the emperor and other courtiers for their wrongful deeds and criticised their misdeeds fearlessly. We should, therefore, have expected from him that if such a misfortune had fallen upon a girl and the story was current in his days, he would have recorded it in his work. Similarly, Khafi Khan, who was an arch-enemy of Jahangir and seldom hesitated relating events not in favour of the emperor, is also silent in the matter. Had such an incidence taken place involving Jahangir, he would have certainly taken notice of it. The other near-contemporary source was Wala-e-Daghistani who has recorded several stories of Jahangir's romances and frivolities except the romance of Anarkali. The other contemporary and very important source is his own diary, the Tuzuk which contains first hand information about his life. He has described, without prejudice, facts about himself and has not concealed his faults. However, he has not said a single word about Anarkali or her tragic story.

Further, it has been related that the girl was sent to the Mughal court at Lahore by Raja Man Singh from Kabul when he was the governor of that province. Now we are told that Raja Man Singh was sent to Kabul in the year 993/1585 on the death of prince Muhammad Hakim and stayed there for about three years. He returned to the capital in 1587. During these years, Akbar was no doubt staying at Lahore in connection with his campaigns in the north i.e. Kashmir, Qandahar, etc. The starting point of the story, therefore, sets in historical perspective, but gives way immediately when we try to corroborate it with the first date inscribed on the marble cenotaph i.e. 1008/1599 supposed to be the date of her death. While it may be surmised that the girl was sent by Man Singh to the imperial court at Lahore, the principal event which took the very life of the unfortunate girl, does not stand the test of historical analysis, because at the time when the incident is said to have taken place, both the emperor as well as the prince were far away from the scene. According to the principal authorities of the period, Akbar left Lahore for Agra on November 6, 1598 and from there proceeded to Deccan on September 16, 1599 while prince Salim was busy in an expedition against Mewar from where he proceeded to Allahabad. Thus both the main actors of the drama were far away from that scene and did not meet each other during the period between 1007 and 1011/1598-1602. Further, it has been said that, it was in the Shish Mahal. Now the fact remains that no such palace existed in the fort at this time as the palace referred to was erected by Shah Jahan in 1041/1631, at least 33 years after the occurrence of the event.

The sum total of the above discussion, therefore, is that there is nothing to prove that there ever existed a slave girl named Anarkali in the Mughal Harem who was executed under the order of the emperor, Akbar on the pretext that she had a love affair with prince Salim, and that a magnificent tomb like the one under discussion was erected by his son and successor, Jahangir. It is evidently clear that the romantic story has been built up gradually by various fiction writers on a casual mention of a street-gossip recorded by an ignorant English traveller. Every author made it spicy and, consequently it gained a fabulous flavour and remained a favourite subject for later story tellers, novelists and movie makers. The uneven recording of the factual details of these writers is itself an evidence that it is nothing but a fiction, far away from sober history.

Leaving aside the controversy of personage lying buried, architecturally the tomb is an imposing structure representing the earlier phase of the development of Mughals architecture in the subcontinent.

The tomb was constructed in the midst of a garden on the bank of the river. This is in line with the usual paraphernalia of a garden-tomb inactive of the Mughal period. The perimeter wall, the gateway and the garden within it no longer exist, the original features of the tomb specially the panelled lime plaster and fresco decoration have also been encroached, misuse, and modern repairs and renovation have practically done away with anything. Some of the alcoves and small rooms on 1st floor still have the original fresco work which is worth seeing.

The tomb, a huge and massive structure created in brick tiles laid in lime mortar, is octagonal in plan with sides, measuring 44 feet and 30 feet 4 inches. It stands in the centre of a 2 ½ feet high octagonal platform, now repaired thoroughly. Each corner of the tomb's octagon has a domed tower, also octagonal on plan, while the main edifice is crowned with a huge double dome placed on a high cylindrical neck or drum. The lower shell of it is constructed in small brick tiles in five stages or rings with a set forward in each case to reduce the thickness of the dome's masonry. Each octagon has a recessed arched opening with a half dome, decorated with three arched-panels and semi-stallactite ornamentation in time plaster. The ornamentation has disappeared.

The interior of the tomb is in two stories i.e. ground and 1st floor, and a spacious gallery runs all along the main central octagon. These modifications were made when the church attendance inward and more space was required to seat those attending on Sundays etc. The dome of the tomb is double

The marble cenotaph is a monolith hewn from the rock in the shape of a single block seven feet in length, and one foot four inches in width, exclusive of the plinth which has of course, disappeared as the cenotaph was removed from its original place.

The marble sarcophagus is one of the remarkable specimen of artwork of Mughal period. It has a marked influence of the art of calligraphy brought over to the Subcontinent from Iran during the period. It is noteworthy that until the earlier days of Akbar's reign, Naskh was generally used for monumental calligraphy and very few specimens of Nasta'liq of this period are known to exist. The simple but elegant style was, later on, developed into more ornate stone inlay and the pietra dura, the more prominent specimens being at the tombs and mausolea of Jahangir, Shah Jahan, Jahan Ara, Asif Khan, etc.

As usual with many religious monuments of the Muslim period of the Subcontinent, the tomb of Anarkali was also condemned to the desecrated use during the Sikh period. In 1194/1780, when Lahore was occupied by the three Sikh Sirdars for loot and arsonry, the tomb was used as a 'thana' where a band of soldiers belonging to Sirdar Sobha Singh, the third of the above trio, remained encamped. It has been reported that at one time during a military scuffle between the two Sikh Sirdars, the 'thana' was bombarded and its 'thanedar' was killed. Ranjit Singh gave the edifice to his son, Kharak Singh, for his residence. After some time, it was allotted to M. Ventura, an Italian Officer of the Sikh army who converted it into his private residence. According to Latif: Adjacent to it was the handsome house of M. Allard, and in front of it, a parade ground intervening, were the lines of the Sikh Regiments and battalions under the orders of the French Officers. This statement shows that the formal Mughal Garden surrounding the tomb had by that time disappeared and a parade ground had taken its place.

The tomb is now used as Archival Repository of the Punjab Government. Tourists are allowed to see the tomb during visiting tours, inspite of the fact that it is located in Secretariat. A small archival Museum has also been set up by the Archives Department for the interest of visitors which mostly contains documents, portraits, pictures, prints, sketches and some other historical documents like the final receipt for payment of Rs. 75 lacs for sale of Kashmir to Maharaja Gulab Singh of Kashmir. A visit to the tomb is really rewarding in terms of seeing documents pertaining to history of Punjab.

THE SAMADHI OF RANJIT SINGH

Opposite to the fort entrance (Shah Burj Gate), to the west, is the Samadhi of Maharaja Ranjit Singh. It is a mixture of Hindu and Muslim architecture, substantially Hindu with Mohammaden details, and is built of stone in plain, unpretending style. The front of the doorway has images of Ganesh, Devi and Brahma, the Hindu deities, cut in red sand-stone. The ceilings are gorgeously decorated with small convex mirrors, set in white cement. The carved marble lotus flower in the central vault, set beneath a canopy, covers the ashes of the great Maharaja, and the smaller flowers of the same description around are in memory of his four wives and seven slave girls, who immolated themselves on the funeral pyre of their deceased lord. The knobs representing the queens, are crowned, while plain knobs mark the sacrifices of the equally devoted but less legal wives, the slave girls. Two more knobs are in honor of two pigeons who, being accidentally enveloped in the great mass of flames, were burnt, and are given the honor of satti, or self-sacrifice.

The marble Baradari of Devi in one of the chambers, was the property of Maharani Jindan, mother of Dulip Singh, who, on her removal from Lahore, made a gift of it to the Samadhi. In the small niches of the side walls are placed the marble images of the Hindu gods, which are worshipped by the disciples of the Guru.

The building was commenced by Kharak Singh, but his untimely death prevented him from completing it. Sher Singh executed part of the work, but it could not be finished until the latter period of Dulip Singh's reign. The marble arches of the interior were once in a dangerous state, but were clamped with iron, and strengthened with fresh materials, under order of Sir Donald Macleod, late Lieutenant-Governor of Punjab. Within the enclosure of the Samadhi long bearded Sikh priests will be found reading the Granth, or the Sikh scriptures, over which is reverentially waved a chauri, or fan of peacock-feathers, an emblem of sanctity. The Sitar, so fondly heard by Nanak from his faithful disciple Mardana, is played, and sacred hymns, describing the deeds of their valorous Gurus, are sung with fervor and enthusiasm. The whole thing is done in a most orderly way; the chantings are heard with absorbing attention, and solemn silence is observed throughout the proceedings. The recitals over, the voluminous books are carefully wrapped up in cases of rich silk, and the assembly departs, favourably impressed with the sacred scene.

Two small domed buildings on the further side of the mausoleum are the memorials of Kharak Singh, the son, and Nao Nihal Singh, the grandson, of the Maharaja.

Below the Samadhi of Ranjit Singh, by the side of the road leading from the Roshnai Gate to the external plain, is the Shrine of Arjun Mal, the fifth Sikh Guru, and the compiler of the "Adi Granth", which now forms the principal portion of the Sikh scriptures.

After partition of India, due to very cordial relations, with Sikh community the place on arrival of 'Yatris' from India is the 1st point of visit. The adjoining area towards north has been made a sports stadium. On various religious days there is lot of hustle bustle especially by the Sikh community. The Roshani Gate which is the entry from the Hazuri Bagh is no longer in use and probably closed for security reasons. The Samadhi is a religious place of Sikh visitors.

WAZIR KHAN MOSQUE

Entering from Dehli Darwaza of old city, at about two furlongs, one finds the famous Wazir Khan Mosque. Now encircled on all sides by residential quarters, shops, streets and Bazars. The mosque of Wazir Khan is important not only because it is mosque and the largest mosque within the city, but because of its contribution to the tile decorations of the period of Shah Jahan. Wazir Khan was the title taken in later life by Sheikh Ilm-ud-Din, born in Chiniot in the Jhang District. Educated in medicine at Dehli, he was employed in the household of Shah Jahan when he was still Prince Khurram; he was afterwards raised by the Emperor to the dignity of Governor of the Punjab. He founded the mosque, endowing it with certain shops and lands for its maintenance and support.

The mosque is in the Perso-Mughal style; the minars, some hundred feet in height, are of particular grace. But the chief virtue of the building lies in its decorative tile work. The brick walls were originally covered with a fine chunam plaster. Which must have formed a far better setting to the tile work than the brick surface now exposed. The tiles afford many examples of the technique employed in the later period of tile decoration, in which different colours were cut to shape, in the manner of the coloured glass in a stained glass window, and then embedded in a matrix of mortar.

The mosque was founded in 1044 A. H. or 1634 A. D. by (Sheikh 'Ilm-ud-Din Ansari, son of Sheikh Abdul Latif, son of Sheikh Hisam-ud-Din, a resident of Chiniot, now in the Jhang district, who rose to the rank of Minister in the reign of Shah Jahan, with a command of 7000 and the title of) Wazir Khan. He entered the service of Prince Khurram (Shah Jahan), while the latter was still a prince. Subsequently, he became Superintendent of the royal kitchen (Mir Saman), and was afterwards created a Diwan under the Prince. The Prince was so much pleased with the Hakim's devotion to duty and his superior qualifications, that, soon after ascending the throne, he raised him to the dignity of Viceroy of the Punjab. He was physician royal, and treated the members of the royal household with a success which tended to raise him greatly in the estimation of his royal master.

Students of the art of painting are often seen copying these decorations on the spot, as a sort of exercise, which is proof of the high skill and taste of the artists who designed the work. The appearance of life and freshness in the variety and profusion of the colouring, as also the excellence and richness of the design, render these decorations the admiration of the spectator.

As a proof of the unrivalled skill, beauty and excellence of the painted decorations in the interior of wazir Khan's mosque, it may be interesting to note that the advanced students of the Mayo School of Arts, Lahore, were taught lessons from those designs by reproducing them on paper. So eminent an authority as Mr. J. L. Kipling, Principal of the institution, writes of the decoration of Wazir Khan's mosque, in his official report:- "This beautiful building is in itself a school of design; but year by year less attention seems to be paid to its maintenance, and the painted work is in a dilapidated state of neglect. Under these circumstances, it seems of the highest importance to secure careful copies for preservation in the Museum and School, and there could be no better training for our young decorators. It is a matter for real regret that we should be so wanting in public spirit as to suffer this most valuable gift of the late Wazir of Shah Jahan to the citizens of Lahore to fall to pieces."

It is remarkable for the profusion and excellence of the inlaid pottery decorations in the panelling of the walls. Local legend say that artists were sent for expressly from China to execute the work; but there is no authority for this association, nor is there any trace of Chinese style in either the design or the execution. Its origin is manifestly Persian. It will be observed that in these arabesques each leaf and each detached portion of the white ground is a separate piece of pot or tile, and that the work is strictly inlay and not painted decoration, although it appears so. The panels of pottery are set in hard mortar.

In the mosque itself are some very good specimens of Perso-Indian arabesque painting on the smooth chunam walls. This work, which is very freely painted and good in style, is true fresco painting, the buono fresco of the Italians, and, like the inlaid ceramic work, is no longer practised, modern native decoration being usually fresco or mere distemper painting. The reason of this is that there has been no demand for this kind of work for many years. Though the builder was a native of the Punjab, the style is more Perso-Mughal and less Indian than that of any other building in the city. Since Masjid Wazir Khan is the master piece of Architecture in the city of Lahore it is necessary that its plan, the interior and general features are discussed slightly in detail.

The plan of the mosque is a perfect rectangle with its sides 280 by 160 feet. The Qibla wall contains a niche in its centre which is projected outside the back wall.

The façade of the main entrance on the eastern side of the mosque, is covered with multi-coloured glazed tiles (Kashi Kari) and inscriptions headed by "Kalima" on its lintel alongwith the date (1045/1635) of its final completion. There are other inscription on its right and left wings. The main entrances's interior is beautifully arranged on the right and left, with turrets and balconies which have made this whole construction imposing indeed.

93

Through the entrance within the centre of the corridor's western side, we enter the courtyard of the mosque itself which is a huge rectangle and consists of an upper and a lower part which is almost square in shape, contains a water basin for ablution, as well as the tomb of Shaikh Ishaq Gazruni towards the south-west. But the visitor immediately looks at the façade of the prayer chamber of the mosque towards the west which may be called the main part of the mosque.

It consists of five porticoes, the central one of which is larger and higher than the others on its right and left and is architecturally called the fronton of the mosque.

The prayer chamber consists of five porticoes on its façade and each portico carries a dome over it, which is cusped in shape and double in construction. The half-domed front of the central portico and the Mehrab in the centre of the back wall are connected with the central dome. The central-niche of the mosque is also projected outside the back wall, which is quite evident in the plan of the mosque. Particularly the prayer chamber of the mosque's plan will show that on its northern and southern ends separate apartments have been made which are quite independent so that the prayers within the mosque may not be disturbed by street noise.

A prominent feature of the mosque is its four minarets which stand on the four corners of the court-yard. The stair-cases built within them carry one to their tops. They are erected on square bases and about the middle of their height they assume in octagonal shape which continues up to the canopies resting on projecting balconies and having domes over them. They are also artistically decorated with "Kashi Kari" harmonising with the embellishment of the rest of mosque.

The floor of this mosque from its entrance to its back wall is very artistically paved throughout, the bricks being set in very beautiful geometrical patterns, with their thin edges being visible. The design which is a geometrical layout harmonises with the entire decorative scheme of the mosque. These geometrical patterns require a careful study which will also manifest other points of the mosque's set-up. In short, the floor gives an additional charm and beauty to the entire building of the mosque.

The material used in the construction of the Mosque is a small brick generally used by the Mughals when stone was, not obtainable or, too costly (at least in Lahore). The only stone in the building is used for brackets and some of the fretwork "pinjra". The walls were coated with plaster 'chunam' and faced with a finely-sifted quality of the same material tooled to a marble-like surface and coloured. All the external plaster work was coloured, a rich Indian red, in true fresco, and the surface afterwards picked out with white lines in the similitude of the small bricks beneath. The extreme severity of the lines of the building is relieved by the division of the surfaces into slightly sunk rectangular panels, alternately vertical and horizontal, the vertical panels having usually an inner panel with arched head, or the more florid cusped 'mehrab'. These panels, where they are exposed to the weather, are generally inlaid with 'Kashi', the effect of which must have been very fine when the setting of deep red plaster of the walls was intact. The origin of this variety of 'kashi' in the Punjab seems obscure and the method of manufacture uncertain.

The façade of the sanctuary is practically covered with 'Kashi' and is divided into the usual oblong panels. A beautiful border is carried rectangularly round the centre archway, and inscriptions in Persian characters occur in an outer border, in a long panel over the archway, and in horizontal panels along the upper portions of the lower walls to right and left. The spandrels are filled in with extremely fine designs. A 'mudakhal' pattern runs along the parapet of this façade, up the sides of the heightened central portion and round the lower gallery of the 'Minars'. The two panels on right and left of the central archway bear inscriptions, as do also the two panels on each side between the smaller arches.

The decorative work covering the western elevation of the vestibule building is a beautiful treatment of the small domes over the kiosks.

"The design of the 'minars' is particularly good. The division of the height into its several parts is most admirable. From above the parapet of the square, strong base rises on the octagonal shaft-the change from square to octagon giving a degree of lightness, while the division of the surface into rectangular panels suggest rigidity. Again the shaft rises from above a dividing band to geometrical pattern and, still preserving its octagonal section, is cleverly divided into sixteen narrow pointed panels, from the heads of which spring a most graceful tracery of "alub kari" or pendentive work drooping gently outwards to carry the gallery with richly coloured borders and "pinjra" parapet. From the gallery rises an elegant kiosk with sloping caves supporting first an octagonal drum, and above this a circular one which curves slightly outwards to support the pointed and ribbed dome with its lotus final.

The internal decoration is extremely rich and elaborate and is executed in fresco on an exquisitely fine 'chunam' surface. The painting demanding first attention is the covering of the internal walls and cupolas of the sanctuary. Round the lower part of all these walls runs a dado four feet in height, of arabesque design, usually surrounded at each change of surface-level by a gracefully flowing floral border and narrow bands of plain colour. Monotony is avoided by frequent variation in the arabesque patterns, and while all are characterised by grace and admirable discretion, one pattern is particularly fine. The field is deep ochre ("old gold') with a bold strapping superposed in rich red, relieved at each edge by a white line, which is again divided from the field by a fine black line. At certain points where the strapping interlaces, it passes through cartouches of pale natural blue relieved by white and black lines in the same manner as is the strapping. Simple leaves and flowers trail graceful along the straps; and garlands on the blue cartouches encircle the intersections, passing over the under. The deep yellow field, appearing as beautifully shaped panels beneath the plane of the strap work, bears pink naturalistic iris plants, and conventional rose-like flowers with leaves. The floral border is in naturalistic colours on a deep purple-brown ground, and is divided from the filling by narrow bands of pink and green, with white lines between. Many of the white lines in borders and strapping are drawn in agraffito, and so are saved from any possibility of crudeness.

Above the dado, the walls are divided into rectangular panels, alternately horizontal and vertical, the vertical ones having the cusped Persian mehrab shape painted within them, and those which are horizontal having both ends similarly shaped. The spandrils so formed are usually in deep colouring dark red or blue or other rich ground, with conventional flowing patterns of flowers and leaves in naturalistic tints. The field of the upright panels usually bears a finely drawn, gracefully growing flower, or group of flowers, issuing from conventionally indicated grassy ground or from a very chinese 'martoban' or vase. Wherever the 'martoban' is used, it is used, and treated as though copied from blue and white pottery, and is generally standing in a kind of 'chilamchi' or bowl, with a thin stem. The leaves and flowers are tinted in quasi-natural colours, with a certain amount of shading and variety of tone, and are always freely outlined and "fibred" with black. On the background frequently float Persian clouds.

The variety of flowers introduced to these designs, and the appreciation and 'verve' with which they are drawn is remarkable, and shows what lovers of flowers the Mughals were. One sees this, too, constantly expressed in their illuminated books, in their landscape and garden subjects occurring in domestic mural paintings, and more particularly in the elaborately constructed flower-beds in their 'baghs' and around their tombs.

The cupolas are divided into gracefully designed panels, in which the balance of rich and delicate colouring is most admirably preserved, and the applicability or fitness of the enrichment never ignored. The beauty of the panelling is well shown in the right half of panels and the balance of colour, approximately, in the opposite half. The effect of the decoration of these cupolas and walls in the soft warm glow of the light reflected from the sun-lit pavement without is very beautiful, strongly suggesting tapestry. The pavement within the sanctuary was probably covered with an extremely hard, deep, maroon-coloured cement, and in the early part of the day, when the sun strikes under the arches, this would have lent an added richness to the colour within; but, as the heat of the day increases, the reflection draws gradually away, permitting cooler tones to sooth the heated bodies of those who seek shade and peace within the sacred precincts.   To an artistic temperament there is a wonderful fascination in watching the great shadows, towards evening, quenching the glowing sunlight as they glide over the quadrangle.   The cool band projected by the tall south-east minar, stretches out over the pavement and meeting the circumscribing wall, bends up and presently over it, to be broken into fantastic shapes as it makes its way across the endless expanse of terraced house-tops of the city.   When the broad shadow of the sanctuary facade steadily pursuing but ever losing ground, steeps the base of the opposite minar in purple grey, the 'kashi' jewels high above glint in the ruddy light of the sinking sun like the scintillations of a glorious opal.   Then as the call to prayers swells out throbbing over the seething bazars, and good Muslims begin to enter barefooted at the low archway, one feels that it is only where the sun is most fearsome that its potency can provide such a background, and that the most picturesque human conceptions can find such fitting concrete expression.

This practice of embellishing mosques with the sacred texts was in practice from the very beginning.   However, the display of verses on the walls of the Wazir Khan Mosque stretches from its main entrance to the hindmost wall of the praying chamber.   This whole display is a fine specimen of Islamic calligraphy harmonizing with the general scheme of decoration.

The façade of the main eastern gateways; central part's upper lintel over the central arch bears the 'kalima' in 'nasta'liq' style of writing along with the date A.H. 1045/1635 A.D. when the mosque was finally completed. Similarly on its right and left, the rectangular panels bear the name of Emperor Shah Jahan, during whose reign this mosque was built and the year of its foundation is noted in chronological Persian writings. To conclude, it is generally remarked that it is one of the two best finished mosques in the world; the other is Masjid-i-Shah, at Isphan.

THE SHALAMAR GARDENS

About three miles east of old Lahore city is the renowned and delightful garden of Shah Jahan, the Shalamar, or "House of Joy," most appropriately called the Versailles of the Punjab. The garden is squeezed by thickly populated private housing colonies which have totally spoiled the locale of a Mughal garden with a typical environ. But it is still a magnificent remnant of Mughal grandeur, in form an oblong parallelogram, surrounded by a high wall of brick work, 1,200 paces in length and 800 in breadth, with three successive terraces, raised one above the level of the other by a height of 12 or 15 feet, the whole area of the garden covering 80 acres more or less. A canal, brought from a great distance used to intersect this beautiful garden and discharge itself in the middle terrace into a large marble basin: from this basin and from the canal rise 450 fountains which throw up water that is subsequently received into marble tanks, the profuse discharge of water in this way serving to render the atmosphere deliciously cool and pleasant. On the upper terrace is a substantial pillared marble kiosk, or arcaded pavilion (Baradari) open on all sides, and rendered delightful by a string of jets d' eau in front, and some on the lower terraces, which play over a cistern crossed by narrow marble bridges in miniature. In the centre is a reservoir, bordered by an elaborate coping, and a cascade falls into it over a slope of white marble screen corrugated in an ornamental carved diaper. Down this the water ripples into a pond below, whence, falling into another reservoir, it passes to the extremity of the garden. The fountains, when playing, not only add to the picturesqueness of the scene, but have the effect of sensibly diminishing the heat. Pavilions and other buildings are scattered about in various places. The alcoves and summer-houses are of marble and red stone, and tastefully designed.

We do not know the derivation and meaning of the name and the date at which it was first used. We find no mention of the word Shalamar before the time of Nadir Shah and it is commonly understood to mean the "House of Joy." The gardens comprised 80 acres of land surrounded by a high wall. The original entrances were the gateways through the east and west wall of the lower terrace. The higher terrace was reserved for the ladies of the Emperor's Palace and the present entrance from the   G. T. road was constructed after annexation, in 1849 through the sleeping apartments of the Royal harem. The edge of the higher terrace was protected by a high screen of latticed marble. It was death for any man to pass this and the privacy of the harem was thus secured during Mughal period. A Baradari or open pavilion of marble stood in the middle of the screen and looked over an ornamental tank flanked by small marble pavilions. To the right of the Baradari, and near it on the higher level, stands a small isolated building erected by Ranjit Singh and used for the accommodation of the English traveller Moorcroft, when, in 1820, he passed through Lahore on his way to Ladakh under this is a "tah-khana" or under-ground room connected with a well and used as a refuge in summer from the blazing heat. The tank and its pavilion are raised above the second main level of the gardens. To the lower level men were admitted and here the Emperor held his court and transacted business.

Throughout the length of the gardens runs a broad water channel flanked with brick pavements and on both the main levels there are cross channels. In these and other pavements of the gardens, as well as in the platform of the central tank, the old brick work deserves notice. All the old buildings in Lahore are distinguished by the use of small bricks of specially good quality and often very aritstically arranged. The water passes uder the Baradari and falls over marble indentations in a minature waterfall. In front of this is a fine marble throne. On the further side of the tank are two small pavilions and between them is an arrangement, known as the "Sawan Bhadon" a name which recalls the refreshing rains of July and August. This gives a charming effect for an illumination. The water was made to fall to the lower level of the gardens over rows of pigeon holes in each of which was a coloured light; these pigeon holes cover three sides of a marble well of which the fourth side is open towards the lower terrace; fountains played at the bottom of the well; and the illumination was enjoyed from the lower terrace.

There are pavilions along the side walls and that which contains the Emperor's bath is worth inspection. It is the pavilion crowned with a sandstone dome which from the central Baradari can be seen to the right of the upper terrace. It contains a number of rooms between the levels of the terraces arranged as baths and apartments with apparatus for heating water and for working fountains. The rooms retain traces of their old wall paintings. Another pavilion on the same side as the bath is also of interest. It is that in the middle of the upper terrace wall. It contained spacious rooms through which is approached an annexe of the main gardens-a fairly extensive walled enclosure. This is known as the Naqqar Khana and is said to have been used for the accommodation of the musicians and officials who accompanied the Emperor to Shalamar, but from its situation on the upper level it is conjectured that it was used by the women attached to the court.

The whole surface of the garden was covered with trees but in later times these were allowed to degenerate into a dense jungle of mangoes. The income derived from the sale of their fruit was an important perquisite of a hereditary Gardener. The trees were thinned out by Sir Charles Rivaz and charming vistas thus opened. The gardens, however, retain little of their Mughal magnificence for Ranjit Singh removed most of their marble, including the balustrade of the upper level, the decorations of the Baradari, and the metal work of the 450 fountains which play in the water channels and tank. But it is to his credit that finding the gardens in a state of utter neglect and the water channels and tank filled with rubbish, in 1805 he cleaned the place and put it into decent order, replacing the despoiled marbles of the Baradari with stucco.

The charm of these gardens lies in their water, and to supply this elaborate arrangements were necessary. We still use the means devised by Ali Mardan Khan to give the water the head necessary to enable the fountains to play. He brought the water from the Ravi by the Hasli Canal, 80 miles in length- to large cisterns whence it was lifted into reservoirs. But, well water had been used for the fountians when canal water had not been available. Two wells were drawn upon. These were remarkable specimens of the use of the Persian wheel. It is the Persian wheel on which the peasantry of the Punjab largely relied for their irrigation in those times, but they were generally able to work only one wheel in a well, or two at most. The wells which watered Shalamar had such a capacity that twelve wheels at once could be worked in each. Tube wells later replaced the wells. The wells were a few paces outside the gardens and approached through a small door to the right of the pavilion opposite and corresponding to the Emperor's bath. Near it were the reservoirs to which the water was originally lifted by a number of Persian wheels. Another set of reservoirs existed on G. T. road just beyond the present entrance to the gardens and on the opposite side of the road. For sometime the water supply was obtained from the Bari Doab Canal passing through Lahore in later years.

Shalamar is still the scene of a very crowded Lahore spring fair known as the "Mela Chiragan." The whole place and its surroundings then swarned with booths for sweetmeats, cooked foods, drinks and other refreshments; toys and gaudy trifles for personal adornment are exposed for sale; wrestlers, conjurers, snake charmers and troops of caterers for the amusement of the public draw interested and amused audiences. This fair is now arranged outside the Garden around the mausoleum of Madho Lal Husain and on roads etc. But it has lost the big 'Halla Gulla' without its premises. Usually, however, the gardens were a quiet pleasant resort to which one could escape for a few hours from the stress and strain of life in the busy Metropolis. But they form a magnificent setting for ceremonials and were particularly used for this purpose when the late Emperor, Edward the Seventh, and Emperor, George the Fifth, King of Iran, President of Turkey and Premier of China visited Lahore. The broad margins of the water channels and the sides and causeways of the tank before the Baradari were covered with thousands and thousands of "chirags"-the little open earthenware oil lamp of the country, whose tiny speck of soft light is a means of illumination the most effective in the world. Chirags also picked out the Baradari and other building and the trees were hung with lights. Fireworks displayed before the tank doubled their effect by reflection, and the jets of the fountains all at play sparkled with fairy brilliance.

Before 1947, the garden was the favourite resort of the European community of Lahore for fetes, picnics and other parties of various kinds. The grounds were, on such occasions, artistically laid out with walks, flower beds and promenades; the fountains play; the branches are tastefully formed into graceful arches over the walks. The illuminations had a most admirable effect on the luxuriant foliage of the mango and orange trees, and their bright reflections in the watery sheets below spread like so many transparent mirrors, constitute a magic scene. The chateau glittering with colored lamps, seems like a fairy palace, the trees, the lakes, the paths, the roofs of the marble structures, all shimmering with variegated lights. The fireworks, diffused in most singular lights and colors, float the garden in an ocean of flame.

The gardens, or the royal pleasure grounds of Shalamar, were laid out in the sixth year of Shah Jahan's reign, or in 1634 A. D., after the plan of the royal gardens in Kashmir, by orders of the Emperor, under the management of Khalilullah Khan. The canal, or Hasli, to irrigate the gardens was brought from Madhupur, at the expense of two Lacs of rupees. It was the combined work of Ali Mardan Khan, the great canal engineer, and Mulla Ala-ul-Mulk. The cost of the gardens and the building attached to it was six Lacs of rupees, and they were laid and constructed in one year, five months, and four days. Mulla Abdul Hamid, Lahori, in his excellent work the Badshahnama, gives, the following interesting particulars of the first State visit of the Emperor to these gardens. "It having been represented to His Majesty that the gardens, the management of which had been entrusted to Khalilullah Khan, had been finished, the royal astrologers were ordered to fix an auspicious hour for the visit of the august sovereign. Accordingly, the 7th of Shaban 1052 A. H. was fixed as the date of the royal visit. His Majesty honored the gardens with a visit on that day, and was highly pleased with the scene he witnessed. The omerahs and grandees of State offered their congratulations, while all joined in prayers for the duration of the Imperial grandeur. Multitudes of intelligent and wise men who were present before His Imperial Majesty, and who had seen Rome, Iraq and Mawar-un-Nahar, represented to him that a garden such as this had never to this date been constructed, or seen, or even talked of by any body." "So many edifices," adds Abdul Hamid, "were constructed in this garden, that, whenever it pleases the Emperor to pay a visit to it with the Royal Hare, who remain with him at Lahore the capital (Dar-us-Sltanat), the necessity of pitching tents is avoided." Towards the east are, the Royal Bath-Rooms. These consist of four arched chambers, with beautiful reservoirs, which can be heated by fire place outside the rooms to the east.

The garden is divided into two divisions, the first being called Farah Bakhsh, and the second, which includes the middle and the third terraces, Fyz Bakhsh.

During the troublous days of Ahmad Shah, the Sikhs laid their ruthless hands on this magnificent garden, and robbed it of much of its decorative works. A costly pavilion of a gate was removed by Lehna Singh, one of the three rulers of Lahore, and sold for Rs.24,000 to stone-polishers in the city. Ranjit Singh barbarously defaced the gardens by removing a large portion of the marble embellishments, to decorate his new constructions at the favorite religious capital of Amritsar, and the contiguous fortress of Govindgrah. The marble pavilions, by the central reservoir, were used in adorning the Ram Bagh of Amritsar, and, in their stead, structures of brick and whitewash were substituted.

Emperor Shah Jahan built the Shalamar Gardens for the pleasure of the royal household, who often stayed here for days or weeks at a time. In design, it conforms to the classic Mughal conception of the perfect garden and consists of three terraces of straight, shaded walks set around a perfectly symmetrical arrangement of ponds, fountains and marble pavilions, all surrounded by flower beds and fruit trees and enclosed within a wall. The garden was designed to be entered from the lower terrace, which was opened to distinguished members of the public. Honoured guests then moved against the flow of the cool waters to discover new and greater delights at the middle terrace, which was used for entertaining. Only intimates of the royal family were permitted to experience the supreme serenity of the upper terrace, the royal inner sanctum.

These days, visitors troop straight on to the upper terrace from the Grand Trunk Road which has been established as entry, the other being not in use. The garden terrace is divided into quarters by ponds splashed with fountains and has nine buildings, including the octagonal towers at each corner of the building's three rooms, the walls and ceilings of which were once covered with frescos, opening on to a wide verandah overlooking the garden through five gracefully cusped arches.

The emperor's sleeping quarters are in the centre of the eastern wall, now crumbling across from the Hall of Public Audience, which gets through the wall and out of the garden. The emperor walked through this hall daily to show himself to the public gathered in a separate walled garden outside. The arcaded pavilion on the northern side of the terrace was the Hall, which was once covered with frescos and used for ceremonial functions. The little house in the northeast quarter, built by the Sikhs earlier in the 19th century, was used as a guest house. William Moorcroft, the prodigious English explorer, stayed here (in 1820).

The middle terrace is four meters (13 feet) down and reached by two flights of steps on either side of the Hall. Between them, a cascade carries water down from the upper ponds to the great central pond, a broad square of water upon which plays 150 fountains. Between the cascade and the pond, and surrounded by a marble railing, is the emperor's marble throne, where he sat in the moonlight listening to his musicians play and watching the girls dance.

Two pavilions on either side of a waterfall guard the steps between the middle and lower terraces. In rows along the marble wall behind the waterfall are hundreds of little cusped niches. Flowers in golden vases occupied them by day, and lamps by night, so that, when viewed from the lower terrace through a double row of five cusped arches, the waterfall was a shimmering sheet of light.

The lower terrace, the least exciting, has two gates decorated with glazed-tile mosaics, two corner towers and a Hall of Private Audience once decorated with white marble and frescoes.

The hydraulic system followed for the Shalamar gardens is complicated as well as interesting. As the natural physiography of the plains, lacks springs and the natural gradient, did not provide an adequate quantity of water with desired hydraulic pressure the foremost priority was that of devising means to overcome this difficulty. First of all a spot with just enough height was selected on the left bank of river Ravi before it reached Lahore. The first step undertaken was to branch off a canal from the Ravi. The canal, which came to be known as Shah Nahr or the Royal canal, was designed by Ali Mardan Khan in such a way as to arrange the flow of water upto the southern portion of the Shalamar, considerably higher than the river flowing on its north. Mulla Ala ul Mulk Tuni also helped later to achieve the desired results and "Nahr" was flowing full with water from Madhopur to Lahore. The canal later on came to be known as 'Hassle' canal and finally Shalamar distributory till its closure in 1958 as a result of non-availability of water in pursuance of the Indus water Treaty with India. The water of Shah Nahr was used for two purposes: (i) Irrigation of the complex of gardens including Shalamar, and (ii) filling of the canals of the upper terrace and the main tank in the middle terrace. The same water, now in the upper-terrace canal, was also used to run the 'abshar' – the Central Marble Cascade and separate the fountains of the middle terrace.

The water was also used to irrigate gardens and for filling the first terrace canal to supplement canal water flow. A well, with persian wheel, ensured the constant supply of clear water. An overhead reservoir was constructed which stood at a height of about 25 feet from the bed level of the Ist terrace. The reservoir consisted of two inter-connected tanks. The water lifted from the well was discharged into the main tank meauring 61'-6" x 17' 6". Three holes, each with 4" diameter, transferred the water to the next tank of 17'-6" x 12' 6" dimensions. The latter served as the filtration tank where sand particles with water would settle down. The water then travelled to two chambers, 11'-3" x 7'–2" and 4'–3" x 7'–2" size, through four holes positioned vertically. The depth of all the tanks including the chambers was kept uniform at 4'–6". The reservoirs were built in solid brick masonry and outlets, where provided, have been chiselled out in one-piece of red sand stone Block.

From the western side of the large chamber a 6" dia outlet provided water to the pipe which was downed and kept underground while another such outlet was also placed in the eastern chamber of lesser dimensions.

To feed these fountains two more connections, one on each end of the east west canal, were given. The western connection took its supply, through an aqueduct along the western perimeter wall, from the overhead reservoir situated on west of the uppermost terrace, from where the water supply to the Ist terrace was also augmented as mentioned earlier. A well, located near the north-eastern Burj of the Ist terrace, supplied water to the eastern end via an overhead reservoir and aqueducts running on the perimeter wall.

Coming back to the upper terrace we find that the water supplied from the Shah Nahr multiplied by that discharged into the canal by playing of 105 fountains would not hold itself within desired limits unless channelized properly with precise calculations. The hydraulic engineering achieved another feat by utilizing this surplus water for the running of the main marble cascade and 153 fountains of the middle terrace.

At the end of the Central canal, just near the pavilion, eight feeding points in the form of outlet pipes, four from each side of the channel, were provided for the fountains of the main tank of the middle terrace, "Sawan Bhadon" and eventually for the running of the fountains of the 3rd terrace. The extraordinary thickness of the solid brick masonry has always proved a barrier against ascertaining the exact layout of these pipelines. Their positioning, however, suggests that they pass under or close to the central baradari. Similar difficulties are faced with the central tank of the middle terrace where 152 fountains are arranged in 4 rectangles in an impressive symmetry. The floor of the tank has been laid in a six foot thick solid brick masonry in lime mortar. It, once again, rendered it impossible to know the exact routes of the pipelines laid under the thick and heavy floor. Faced with this difficulty especially during a leakage, archaeologists and conservationists had to seek the help of nuclear scientists to locate these pipelines. The "sealed radiation source" method cleared the picture to some extent. We now surely know that all the fountains of the central tank were interconnected. It was, indeed, also necessary to produce harmony in their playing.

Cascade:- This tank served as the main reservoir to supply water to "Sawan Bhadon" and to the fountains of the lower most terrace. After filling the tank, the water split into two small cascades, on eastern and western sides, and flowing over the "Sawan Bhadon" discharged into the canals of the lower terrace. A part of the water in the central tank was channeled through pipelines to feed the fountains of the 3rd terrace. Eleven pipes served as feeding points for the purpose. The arrangement of these lines was made on a sophisticated and precise plan to make maximum use of the water in the tank. Three pipelines were used to feed 3 parallel rows of fountains in the central canal of the 3rd terrace: four pipes fed the five fountains located in the inner basin of "Sawan Bhadon" while the remaining four pipelines supplied water to two cascades of the "Chini Khana."

The water from the cascades and fountains filled the canals of the 3rd terrace. Its disposal was finally arranged through drains under the Baradari at the northern most end of the central canal. Outside the perimeter wall of the garden, this water was used to irrigate Mahtabi Bagh, a fruit garden, and a large tank situated in it. The surplus water was drained out. This beautiful gift of the Mughal Emperor to the city of Lahore, although used till date is not maintained to the desired level.

THE SONEHRI MASJID

The Sonehri Masjid, or the golden Mosque of Nawab Bhikari Khan, in the Kashmiri Bazar, stands on a masonry platform, about a storey above the level of the road, which it overlooks. It is a remarkably handsome and elegant building, and with smallness of size combines perfect symmetry of form. The original covered entrance is to the south, and the stone steps lead to the court of the mosque; but a gateway, facing the main street was opened to the east. It has contributed much to its beauty and the commanding and the picturesque positon it enjoys. The mosque is built throughout of masonry, and the three arched entrances are covered with three large gilt domes, the centre dome being larger than those on either side. Over the arched entrances is a parapet of small, narrow open arches, surmounted by a row of small ornamental gilt domes. In the middle of the court-yard is a tank, or cistern filled with water for the ablutions of the congregation.

According to Syed Latif, the founder of the mosque was Nawab Syed Bhikari Khan, son of Raushan-ud-Daula Turrabaz Khan, deputy governor of Lahore, during the reign of Muhammad Shah, and the viceroyalty of Mir Moin-ul-Mulk, alias Mir Mannu, the gallant opponent of the Durrani Ahmad Shah. He built the mosque in 1753 A. D. He was a handsome young man, well-versed in the Muslim Fiqah Law, and of pious and amiable dispostion. On the death of Mir Mannu, when his widow, Morad Begum, assumed the reins of government in the name of her infact son, Bhikari Khan enjoyed her full confidence.

The mosque was taken possession of by the Sikhs (Akalis) in the time of the Ranjit Singh. They plastered the floor with cow-dung and placed the Granth, or Sikh holy scriptures, in it. The Muhammadens asked Fakirs Aziz-ud-din and Nur-ud-din to intercede in their behalf with the Maharaja for the restoration of the mosque. Through the good offices of the Fakirs, backed by Gullo Mashki, the favourite water-carrier, who exercised much personal influence over Ranjit Singh, the Maharaja restored the mosque to the Muslims, on the condition that the calls to prayrs were not, to be made loudly, and the income of the shops attached to the Masjid was to be appropriated by the Darbar. The British Government restored these shops to the Muslims, on the recommendation of Deputy Commissioner, Lahore.

THE TOMB OF QUTB-UD-DIN AIBAK

The tomb of Qutb-ud-Din Aibak was accidentally detected from an epitaph lying in a wretched condition in Anarkali area by the archaeologists. It was in a very narrow lane where it was difficult to reach until 1947. It was in the late sixties that the Government of Pakistan after a lot of effort acquired the house which had been, infact, built upon it and the grave had been hidden under balcony of the same. After acquisition and clearing the surrounding houses a new tomb was built and the road named as Aibak Road joining the Hospital road with Anarkali Bazar.

The original tomb was two storeyed high, composed of architectural beauty which was demolished during Sikh period. Constructed in 1970 by the Archaeology Department, Government of Pakistan, the tomb has been built in conformity with Sultanate Style of architecture. The stones used are yellow stones of Thatta which were in vogue during Aibak's time. The monument depicts twenty five models of Qutub Minar which add to the magnificence of the tomb. On the marble slabs are inscribed 'Sura-i-Yasin' in thick and artistic manner.

It may be mentioned in passing that the minar known as Qutub Minar in Dehli, was also built by Aibak. It is a master piece of architecture. Aibak was the first Muslim Monrach from the "Slave Dynasty" who ascended the throne in Lahore on 24th July 1206 A. D. After a brief rule of six years he died of an accident while playing polo.

THE CATHEDRAL OF THE SACRED HEART OF JESUS

This sacred edifice, situated on Lawrence Road, near St. Anthoney's High School consecrated in 1887, is a master-piece in architecture, a product of Beljian talent.

The exterior of the Cathedral with its lofty steeple, massive dome and its turrets is as imposing as the interior is inspring. The belfry steeple, 105 feet high over the entrance stands attended by well proportioned towers enhancing the effect of the steeple. The dome 120 feet high is flanked by four elegant turrets. The whole forms a wonderful and very attractive structure.

If there is one feature more than the other which adds to the general beauty of the interior, it is a fine range of stained glass windows above the High Alter, specially when towards sunset the light thrown through them becomes more subdued. It is a sight which penetrates the soul and invites it to adoration and prayer.

Towards the west of the Cathedral is a set of ten stained glass windows in the Chapel of the Lady, representing the Annunciation, Mary's Glorification in Heaven and her meeting with the Lord on the way to Calvary.

THE CATHEDRAL CHURCH OF THE RESURRECTION

This Cathedral, with elegance of its style and the beauty of structure, is really an ornament of which Lahore can be proud.

Built in 1887 A. D. in English style it is situated on Shahrah-e-Quaid-e-Azam, opposite the High Court. The gigantic structure is made of fine redbrick work and grey stones. The first church ever established in Lahore, was in the reign of the Emperor Akbar which was closed in 1614. It was re-opened but in 1632 was demolished, even though various missions continued to preach. First of all, in 1849 the Baradari of Diwan-i-Khas was fitted and used for Sunday services. Later for sometime Haveli Dhian Singh was also used as church.

The Church and afterwards the Pro-Cathedral of Lahore was located in the Tomb of Anarkali – in the Civil Secretariat of Lahore. An entry in the books of the Cathedral, records that, "the old tomb near the Residency, Anarkali was handed over by the Government to be used as a Church for the performance of the Divine Service, according to the church of England in 1851". On January 24, 1857, it was consecrated as St James Church. After being used for thirty years, it became the Pro-Cathedral of Lahore, until the Cathedral was completed on the Mall.

Mr. J. Oldrid Scott was Architect of this Cathedral. The style of Architecture is Gothic and construction carried out in red brick. The pillars and arches are in grey stone, which is again introduced in many other parts of the walls and in the vaulting of the ceiling. There is some fine carving, in the pillars and arches in the sanctuary and choir, the richest found in the stonework. The brickwork is subdued and blends well with the stonework. The marble floor with its beautiful grey tones was the gift of the Freemason society of Lahore. The entry into the Cathedral is from the porch at the west end.

The Cathedral possesses a number of different memorials including brass and wall tablets, which are of considerable interest. In the Sanctuary, there are two screens of wood panelling which are worth seeing. Besides other dignitaries, it was visited by Her Majesty the Queen Elizabeth II of England. Ms. Merle Jivanandham daughter of Mr. Theodore Phailbus was the architect for a memorial on the entry gate, on the Mall side, in connection with centenary celebrations.

GENERAL POST OFFICE

We have already mentioned elsewhere in this booklet that Anarkali gardens were the site of a Cantonment both during the Sikh and British Period, until 1850-51 when the Cantonment was shifted to Mian Mir area. The market which developed for army officers and their family from Lahori Gate to the defunct old Haillay College building was known as Anarkali bazar. Due to Cantonment and all the official residences most of the offices were located in and around this area which was not only out of the existing walled city but to its close proximity. We have no doubt in the systematic management of the British authorities which was one of the causes of success in extending their empire and exercising their authority over a vast area in India. The Post Office came into existence like many other institutions right in the beginning i.e. in 1849. With reference to commanding of Sikh troops by European Generals like Ventura and M. Allard etc. the Sikh contingents under them had also their barracks in the Anarkali area. These were taken over by the British after formal annexation and one such barracks close to the Tolinton Market, sometimes known as Exhibition place, was converted into a Post Office. This was slightly south-west of the Tolinton market and on the east of Punjab Public Library building, now under the C & W and Irrigation and Power Secretariat building. The Post Office was headed by Mr. T. Clifered as the first Post Master who assumed his charge in Lahore on 2th June 1849 and lived in an old banglaw situated close by. There also stood in the vicinity a small cottage known as Lockland under use of the Punjab Volunteers. Although formally the Post Master of Lahore used to work under the Post Master General of North-western Provinces yet according to early records Dr. John Logan, Governor of Lahore Fort was made responsible for the postal affaris by Sir John Lawrence who looked after the Department until he accompanied Dulip Singh on his departure from Lahore. With the expansion of postal services upto Frontier and Kashmir and Post Master made efforts for as more spacious accommodation which had fallen vacant due to shifting of Cantonment. It is understood that the old barrack was demolished in 1854 for the Secretariat of the Public Work Department and Post office located somewhere in Anarkali.

According to Mr. Thornton the Post Office was in Anarkali near the Central Museum (Exhibition Hall – Tolinton Market) which would mean that if it was shifted from South it could either be on the east or south-east around the present Anarkali Chowk and most probably somewhere around in the existing Commercial Building. It had two branch offices one at the Railway Station and the other within the walled city in Moti Bazar. There were pillar letter boxes which were cleared three times a day for various out-going mails. The post packages were despatched from the Post Office by Government bullock train to at least to 14 places incluidng Kanouj, Fateh Grah, Ferozepur, Dera Doon, Simla, Sialkot, Jhelum, Rawalpindi, Murree, Attock, Nowshera and Peshawar.

During this period while the British established their authority and new offices were coming up major constructions of offices like Civil Secretariat, Commissioner's Office, PWD Secretariat, Chief Court, A. G. Office, Financial Commissioner's Office, Central Telegraph Office etc. etc., took place between 1849 – 1894. According to some old papers in the Archives various proposals were considered for locating the General Post Office at an appropriate place in the city and finally the present piece of land was selected where the building was completed and occupied in 1904, a most central place on the Mall facing High Court and Central Telegraph Office buildings. The existing building was plastered and painted due to lack of attention by the authorities in late '70s but was restored in 1984 particularly its exterior to its pristine beauty. The General Post Office is headed by a Deputy Post Master General under the Post Master General, Lahore with over all control of Director General Pakistan Post Offices, Islamabad. The building is in Anglo-Mughal style and occupies a most imposing place in the heart of modern Lahore.

PUNJAB ASSEMBLY CHAMBERS

This is a magnificent and imposing building with entrances from three main large rustless metal gates. The fountains in the front add to the grandeur of the building. Unlike other modern buildings, the Assembly Chambers have tile roofing in the Western style. The building, with lush green lawns looks like an ornament and is considered one of the best modern buildings of the city.

The foundation stone of the present Punjab Assembly building at Lahore was laid on November 17, 1935 by Sir Jogendir Singh, the then Minister for Agriculture Punjab. It was designed by Mr. Bazel M. Sullivan, the Superintending architect, Punjab. It took 3 years to build. The first session of the Assembly, in the building, was held on 10th November, 1938. Since independence, the present Assembly Building at Lahore has been the permanent seat of the Punjab Assembly and for 15 years as the West Pakistan Assembly. The building is a classical piece of architecture raised in pompous Victorian style during the British period. It has a most imposing gateway facing the Mall. The entrance has typical round supporting pillars with Spanish style roof. The steps and floors are in red-stone. Immediately on entrance comes the lounge and stairways leading up to the Assembly Hall where there are entrances on right and left through lobby. Just opposite to Speakers walkway to his Chamber, is the room of leader of the House and on right side of the Hall is the Governor's Gallery. As already pointed out the building is in semi-circle and both on right and left spacious corridor divides the blocks of room which are occupied by the Ministers and their staff. Downstairs there are offices dealing with the matters pertaining to MPA's, establishment of the Assembly etc. The rooms are centrally air-conditioned and panelled. The Assembly Complex extends over an area of 148 Kanals out of which 118 Kanals are under lawns and open spaces. On the north east of the building there is hotel Falettis. On the east PIA building and WAPDA House. On right side of the Assembly Building there is MPA's Hostel and Al-Flah Building. Just in front of the main gate of the Assembly at a distance of few yards is the Summit Minar.

The present seating arrangement, in the Hall, is designed to accommodate 271 members, including Ministers. In addition, there is speaker's throne, Secretary's Table and the Reporter's table. On the left side of the Speaker's throne, is the Governor's Gallery with 12 seats meant for the visitors of the Governor, and on the right side of the throne is the officers Gallery with 12 seats, meant for the Secretaries to the Government.

MINAR-E-PAKISTAN

The historic parade ground where once flowed the river Ravi with thick forest on its north, where Mughals witnessed the Elephant fights, where Ranjit Singh inspected the Millitary parades and where British had their forces camped, and also used the place as cricket and football ground, is no longer a playground. It is a beautiful park. The "Budha Ravi" an arm of the river Ravi is no longer alive. It is just a storm drain. In the centre of Park there stands a Minar which is commonly called 'Yadgar-e-Pakistan'. This Park which was named Minto Park before partition was named Iqbal Park after the creation of Pakistan.

As creation of Pakistan was a great achievement of the Muslims of the sub-continent 52 years ago so Minar-e-Pakistan which symbolises the spirit of the freedom movement is a unique landmark of Lahore, distinguished in its concept of architecture and beauty.

Lahore has many other landmarks like the Badshahi Mosque, Jahangir's tomb, Shalamar Gardens, Islamic Summit Minar etc, but the majestic Minar-e-Pakistan has its own charm and grandeur which reminds the nation of its great struggle for Independence.

Infact, as might be known Lahore was an important political centre for Pakistan movement in Punjab. On 22nd to 24th of March 1940, the All India Muslim League held a session here, in the Minto Park, where they resolved under the Presidentship of Quaid-e-Azam, Muhammad Ali Jinnah to have a separate homeland, in India, under the name of Pakistan which was to consist of Muslim Majority areas in India. This finally materialized in August, 1947 when Pakistan came into being. It was this event which made the place historically important and a Yadgar was built and the ground converted into a Park to commemorate the event.

The construction of the Minar was entrusted to the Pakistan Day Memorial Committee with late Nasir-ud-din Murath Khan, a Turkish architect, as its member. The foundation stone was laid on 23rd March, 1960, and the memorial completed on 31st October, 1968, at a cost of Rs.7,058,000.

The Minar constructed with different stones obtained from the various parts of Pakistan rests on the base built in the shape of a flower with ten petals. The tower rises from a platform shaped like a five-pointed star enclosed by two crescent-shaped pools that have been lined with green and red marble. The hall is spanned by arches. On the marble slabs in the centre is inscribed brief history in English, Urdu and Bengali of the Pakistan Movement, the Pakistan Resolution together with 99 names of God and verses of Iqbal. The tower has 10 vertical converging slates installed with flower petals, glazed cement domes with sight seeing platforms. The rostrum is in Mughal patterned style.

The design and the constructional pattern of the base and the first four platforms depict the history of the Pakistan Movement through architectural symbol.

The dome is of stainless steel inlaid with fine glass pieces. From here you can have the panoramic view of Lahore.

Parks are laid around the memorial with passages in Mughal pattern floors, and eight fountains on the main to beautify the memorial.

The first storey of the Minar is a circular room finished with marble facing. On this are written the ninety-nine attributes of Allah and verses from the Holy Quran. The text of the Pakistan Resolution and short history of Pakistan Movement has also been detailed. Above this room the Minar rises though stages, to a height of 59 metres. A lift has been provided to go right up to the top which is crowned by a domelet made of stainless steel. The Minar is located on a raised plinth and visited by public on Sundays and holidays. Both political and general public meetings are held on national days in this park. It attracts a large crowed of public especially childrens on holidays. It is rather the only post-partition monument raised by Government in Lahore. On national days the Minar is decorated and profusely illuminated at night.

THE ISLAMIC SUMMIT MINAR

In 1974 history was made in Lahore when the Islamic Summit Conference took place. This was attended by many leaders of Islamic Countries. Such an event surely deserves a minar to be built not only as a memorial but also as a standing inspiration to the followers of the 'Millat'. It is a unique symbol of the Muslim urge for unity of more than 40 countries which gathered for the first time for a truly noble cause.

Renowned Turkish Architect Mr. Vader Balokey designed the Minar. It is 150 feet high with a special block representing the globe, with two more blocks on the top appearing like a crescent with embellishment work and calligraphy.

The Minar, which is located just in front of the Punjab Assembly building, has WAPDA House, a multi-storeyed building, on the east and Al-Flah Plaza on the west. Around the base of Minar there is a Museum located in a few Pyrimidical rooms. The Lawn with an edifice (perpetration) is in its south west with a Holy Quran, written in gold, placed there in. One may regretfully remark that this "Minar" has suppressed the speculation grandeur of the Assembly building.

AL-HAMRA

Lahore is a city with a character. It has a history of over 1000 years and a pre-history going back to about 2000 B. C., when Harappan Civilization was at its peak. It has been variously called the city of tombs and turrets, gardens and now the cultural capital of Pakistan; as it is very closely identified with political and cultural life of the country and vanguard of art in Pakistan. As a centre of arts, crafts, architecture, music, drama and literature it gives a special sense of history. Its features are distinct which have evolved through ages with centuries old traditions of art, music, culture and a unique way of living and life. The city has seen some of the most glorious moments of history while at the same time it stands witness to ravages of omnipotent conquerors and to the debasement of vanquished natives. Each new turn of history has left its marks on the city in the shape of monuments, mosques, mausoleums, in the grandeur of the gardens, gateways and palaces. This historical background has given birth to a mixed culture which flourished in older times within the city as well as in the court. With the turn of times this mixed culture which flourished inside the city has shifted to posh housing societies which have mushroomed in suburbs. But Lahore is a city where the old and the new blend into a complete cultural unity and after the creation of Pakistan and advancement of education and technology a sense of disciplined and organized shape has been given to the field of arts. Although British set the ball rolling in the shape of western education, established schools of arts and crafts, during Pakistan period specialized institutions were established in the form of Arts Councils in some cities of the country. Out of these the culture centre generally known as Alhamra Arts Centre, or Arts Council has emerged as premier national institution of performing arts. It is commonly called Alhamra Arts Council, a place which is known in the city for dramatic performances, exhibitions of paintings, musical concerts, instructions to amateurs in music, fine arts and dance. The place is also known and used for multifarious functions and programmes both from public and private sectors. It is a prestigious centre which also hosts most of the State functions and where troupes and artist delegations from abroad perform.

Just to acquaint the visitor with the background of the organization this most developed Cultural Complex was founded by a private society in December, 1948 with financial assistance of the Punjab Government who also funded acquisition of a private property for the establishment of the institution. The founders among others included Justice S. A. Rehman, Mr. S. S. Jafary, Ms.

Roshan Ara Begum, Madam Noor Jahan, Faiz Ahmad Faiz, Imtiaz Ali Taj, Abdur Rehman Chughtai, and Mr. Khalil Sahafi etc. etc. Originally located in an evacuee bungalow the Council started with exhibitions, theatrical performances and imparting instructions in paintings and music. Various known Ustads and Painters remained associated with the institution. The organization subsisted on the financial assistance from the Provincial and Federal Governments. A stage came when the artists and public felt that there was a need for a proper infrastructure, buildings and equipment for making the place more useful to public as cultural venue. The Government was approached at different times and funds for a modern art centre with buildings for theatre, auditorium, art gallery, lecture rooms etc. demanded. Althought the management of the Arts Council started planning its development projects with the foundation stone laying ceremonies in various times by Kh. Nazim-ud-Din, Field Marshal Muhammad Ayub Khan, General Muhammad Musa and Mr. Muhammad Hanif Ramey but the actual work started somewhere in 1975 which remained suspended for sometime until it was resumed under orders of Lt. Gen. Ghulam Jilani Khan the then Governor of the Punjab. The first phase of the building which consisted of Hall-I, Workshop and some allied facilities became operational in August, 1981. Gen. Jilani Khan, the Governor of Punjab was a keen patron of art and he also approved and funded the second phase of Alhamra Hall-II and the Arts Gallery which became operational in the year 1983 and 1985 respectively. Due to his special acumen for revival of classical music he also allowed funds for Alhamra Hall-III with a conference room and a recording room. Later the Arts Council with the efforts of the Commissioner, (the Chairman) of Arts Council, acquired a new campus on Ferozepur Road, where an Open Air Theatre and auditorium were constructed during the year 1991 under specific orders of the Chief Minister Mian Muhammad Nawaz Sharif. To meet the long outstanding demand for a Permanent Art Gallery the Nawaz Sharif Government also allowed funds for such a building. This gallery was inaugurated in the year 1995. The Late Mr. Anwar Zahid Chief Sectary Punjab laid the foundation stone of this gallery. This is now fully operational with a number of art works on display, mostly by the old masters. The city has gone metropolitan and people have high expectations from the Art centre as little is available on the entertainment side in city for various constraints. But the Arts Council being subsistent on Government grants continues with its bit both on programming and education side. While the fine arts are promoted and patronized free and at the Arts Council's expense, popular theatre by the private producers pays for the facilities and is a major source of income for the institution. A particular class of fading artists and so called connoisseurs of theatre expect some sort of serious theatre at public expense. This is not possible due to financial constraints but the Council does pay, attention to this subject to availability of finances. The Arts Council also caters to the needs of children by having regular puppet theatre weekly for the children of the city. Free exhibitions of paintings both one-man and group shows and programmes on National Days are also held free. In addition regular monthly and bye-monthly invitational programmes of music are also a part of the programming sheet of the Arts Council; purely as a promotional activity.

The building of the Arts Council is in red brick with reclining walls in a semi-Pyramidical shape. The name of the institution of Alhamra was suggested according to some reports by famous artist Abdur Rehman Chughatai probably on the analogy of fascinating name of Ahambra which gloriously stood through Muslim history during their rule in Spain. With its limited resources in financial and material terms Alhamra has done best to meet the Cultural needs of the city. All the visiting troupes from friendly counties under bilateral agreements perform here. This list includes Peoples Republic of China, Korea, Iran, U. K., USA, Egypt, Jordan, Turkey etc. etc. Alhamra is a centre of cultural activities and a lovely institution for its plays, exhibitions, music concerts, State functions, wrangling and the little 'olympian jealousies and frolics of the lovely lot of artists we proudly possess'.

THE SHOPPING CENTRES
AND ANARKALI

The sight-seeing of Lahore is not complete unless one visits Business centres of Lahore. Special mention, therefore, is made of the Shopping Centres so that well-known and important commodities can be bought as a memento, within the walled city which is traditionally visited by outsiders for souvenirs.

The shops in Azam Cloth Market in Shah Alami, Kasera Bazar (Brass and Copper Ware) beyond chowk Rangmahal, behind the Sonehri Masjid and the Landa Babar near Railway Station are all very well equipped with articles worth purchasing. All the same the most noted houses have their sales display depot either on Shahrah-e-Quaid-Azam, or Anarkali Bazar, or Beadon Road, or Liberty Market Gulberg or Main Market, or Fortress Stadium, Lahore.

On Shahrah-e-Quaid-e-Azam, the best shopping places are H. Karim Bakhsh and Sons, The Naqi Market, The Panorama Shopping Plaza, Apwa Cottage Industry, and the Cooperative Handicrafts. In Anarkali, Shaikh Inayat-ullah & Sons and Bano Bazar are worth a visit.

The Landa Bazar is comparable to the Petticoat Lane of London, Portapotese in Rome, and the Sunday Markets in other countires of Europe. Mind you the Landa Bazar is a fashion centre of old Lahore. It is invariably associated with used articles, second-hand imported materials, and other of cheap, exotic commodities. The fame of Landa Bazar has travelled to posh localities of Lahore and secret visits even by fashionable ladies and gentlemen in search of bargains are not infrequent.

The Kasera, Dabbi and Sooha Bazar:- Beyond Rang Mahal Chowk under the shadow of the Sonehri Masjid is the Kasera Bazar, the biggest market for brass and copper wares. In Lahore, there is nothing better or brighter than the Kasera Bazar. The shopkeepers enjoy the experience of displaying their wares. If you don't like brass, they will sell you copper, and if you don't care for copper they will sell you fancy things about bronze and if you still hold on, they will bet on aluminum. Indeed although keen competition is there, the shop keepers will not easily leave you, unless they are convinced that you are not a buying kind. Adjoining Rang Mahal chowk is "Sooha Bazar" where all type of jewellery in Gold and Silver is available and the latest.

With all kinds of people stamping through the bazar which is at no place wider than five steps, it seems that the whole wide world has forgotten all its worries and has squeezed itself into this crowded alley to take part in the breathtaking activity of buying pots and pans and jewellry.

The Mall Shopping stores:- There are quite a few modern shopping stores on the Mall starting from Commercial Building, Insurance Plaza, Dial Singh Mansion, Panorama, Naqi Market, Ferozsons and Alfalh Market. Sang-e-Meel Publications is another name in the publications list which is known for reprinting and publishing books on Lahore in particular and Pakistan Movement. It is located on the Lower Mall between PMG Office – New Hostel of Government College.

Just off the lower Mall Police Station on its back is the Urdu Bazar which is the famous area where only Books both English and Urdu, especially text Books of students are sold at reasonable prices. In many new Bazars and markets there exist book shops especially in the modern colonies outside the city.

The Liberty Market:- There are Main Market and Liberty Market and on the Main boulevard of Gulberg the departmental stores like PACE, and ALFATEH , N.M. STORES, H. KARIM BUX in Liberty Market etc. These are the most modern stores where anything imported or indegnious can be found. The same way there are most modern markets around Fortress Stadium in Lahore Cantt., Model Town, Garden Town, Township, Faisl Town and Iqbal Town, Muslim Town, and Ichra Lahore, have there shopping areas, Samanabad etc. etc. have also local Markets. The most historic, well sought and worth visit is the Anarkali Bazar for which a separate writeup appears elsewhere in this book.

For the last couple of years a new trend is there, of course at the behest of Government, for Sunday markets where, from eatables, and food items to fresh fruit is available. Although these are held in public places without any taxes and the commodities should be cheap yet the greedy shopkeepers fleece the customers, here too, like any place.

The controversial legend of Mughal times regarding the love affair of a slave girl and Prince Saleem is nothing to do with this bazar. This bazar grew and developed upon an area occupied by Sikh Troops under the French Officers and later British forces in the shape of cantonment. Due to this local and foreign blend of influence it became fashionable quarter and its fame travelled beyond Punjab and people all over the sub-continent cherished a wish to see the Anarkali (Lahore). The civil station where the Provincial Secretariat, Revenue and Judicial offices, District Courts, Municipal Offices, the Art College and Museum were located came to be known as Anarkali Cantonment quarter, mainly because of the surrounding residential bungalows of the British officers and barracks of the forces. How and why it was called Anarkali has a background. The legendary tomb of Anarkali was located on the bank of the river and was surrounded by vast gardens encompassing areas referred to above which were known as Anarkali Gardens and hence the locality and settlement developed in these gardens came to be known as Anarkali. The area or bazar before taking the shape of a shopping area for the forces was occupied by prostitutes who were made to shift partly to Risala bazar and partly insite the walled city (Lahori Gate). This bazar is to the south of old walled city across the Circular Road with its Police Station (Lahori Gate) on the right end corner of the Bazar. Its other end crosses the Mall Road leaving Nila Gumbad and old F. C. College on its left, the old Punjab University Campus and Museum on its right and ends around near Kapurthala house with old Police Station of Anarkali on the right, opposite Board of Revenue Building. It is said that when Ranjit Singh came to occupy Lahore in 1799 he first located his troops in the Anarkali gardens. Infact Baradari Wazir Khan now under occupation of Punjab Public Library and National College of Arts, behind the Museum, was also a part of the Anarkali Gardens. The shopping area which developed during cantonment period took the formal shape of a modern bazar which became of a cosmopolitan character in due course.

The bazar bearing the name of Anarkali grew and developed around the land under occupation of British troops. It soon became a fashionable quarter and its fame travelled beyond the confines of the province. Being the most attractive 'native' shopping centre mere entry into it was considered an admission to a higher stratum of society. The rustic youngsters would proudly take round of this bazar to have an idea of how majestic Lahore was, and also to enrapture (or shock) them completely by affording them a sight of fashionable feminine flocks – an incredible vulgarity in those days. The visitors to Lahore were invariably taken to the bazar in the evenings when ladies were mostly busy shopping in the area.

As the country acquired affluence from the new canal colonies, Lahore increasingly attracted rural wealth. Anarkali naturally became richer and more charming in the absence of any other modern bazar with variety and almost all saleable commodities. And those who wanted to be conspicuous thronged the bazar exposing themselves to the jampooning of village-bards and the singers of one-anna poems. In pre-partition days Satirical poems caricaturing their passion for modernity were very common in those days and one frequently heard the poems sung up and down the bazar e.g. "Aa ni Kuryia Shahr diayia tanon Pind the kuri Dikhawan". Anyhow the march of modernity has changed it into a modern shopping centre. Whereas the whole length of the bazar from Lahori Gate to Nila Gumbad before 1947 used to be uniformly owned by Hindus except a few Muslim shops under Muslim ownership only to break monotony.

"Some events, in the past, conferred a distinction on this locality. At one time (Allama) Muhammad Iqbal lived in one of its flats; in 1929 Motilal Nehru saw his son's historic procession passing through it from a balcony over the Bhalla Show Company, near Dehli Muslim Hotel, six Khaksars offered their Asr prayer in the bazar surrounded by a large guard in 1940"

Due to its location being out of the walled city where people's dealings were traditional, the market out of the city due to influence of the foreigners emerged as a modern shopping area where the educated and fashionable would go not only for purchases but for window shopping. Surrounded as it was by the University Hostels, the Arts College, the F. C. College, King Edward Medical College and Mayo Hospital the educated and elite instead moving up the old city would go over for purchases after duty hours accompanied by their families and female members. This educated or elite class was slightly different from the traditional folk i.e. old Lahoris in the walled city and thus a social and class difference. The shopkeepers would accordingly market the latest products brought from the best production centres from all over India alongwith imported items for the well off and new bureaucratic and affluent class. The traders understanding the psychy of their customers had special corners for ladies in respect of their wear and cloth stores for the gents. This gradually caused the younger lot from educational institutions to pay casual visits from the adjoining institutions for shopping as well as exchanging looks with the young females who would otherwise shy away in the lanes of old Lahore. It was customary with students and visitors just to take a round of the busy bazar. The Anarkali bazar would cater to the needs of all the customers in respect of variety of items from Jewellery to Army uniforms. This tradition was so strengthened that every visitor would pay homage to the Anarkali whenever in Lahore. Some openly and some disguised. So much so that a person not less than Prime Minister of India Mr. Atal Behari Vajpai made public his wish in Lahore in 1999 to visit Anarkali where he had sneaked in disguise in late 70s. All said and written, no description can substitute the actual round of the Anarkali bazar which must be visited while in Lahore.

THE MALL ROAD

Prior to their formal annexation of Punjab, the British had detailed their forces in Lahore for the protection of Lahore Darbar and the infant Maharaja Dulip Singh. The Residency at the time was located in the present Civil Secretariat building (Chief Secretary Block) and offices in the Anarkali Tomb. The Anarkali Gardens and adjoining areas were used for stationing the forces. This was not a new as the Sikh forces had also been using the area partly barracks for Sikh soldiers under the command of French Officers. The British troops faced hygiene problem in the absence of proper severage and an epidemic caused death of many soldiers. After a proper study and survey of the causes the authorities decided to take away the Cantonment to the Mian Mir area towards east of city. By 1850-51 the civil station was taking a proper shape which was around the Anarkali Tomb and adjoining area of Baradari of Nawab Wazir Khan, near Anarkali Bazar. The administration, therefore, needed to provide a direct link road form Anarkali civil station to the Mian Mir Cantonment, which area was mostly barren with some bushes here and there. It was with this background, that the present beautiful Mall Road of which we are so justly proud and which is admittedly one of the finest public road in Pakistan, was first aligned in 1851 by Lt. Col. Napier, the Civil Engineer of Lahore who described it as a directed road from Anarkali to Mian Mir. Before execution and construction Col. Napier submitted two alternate estimates of cost. These were (i) Rs.12,544/- and (ii) Rs.10,428/-. The former was for providing "Kankar" throughout on the road and the latter for an under layer to burnt bricks with 'Kankar' surface. Col. Napier was of the view that the better design would be sufficiently durable but in transmitting both these estimates to the Government of the Company, the Board of Administration for the Punjab, observed that they thought that as this road would be a great thoroughfare not only with the Anarkali but also with the old city and it should be more economical in the long run to sanction the higher estimates. Not agreeing with the views of the Board, the Government of India sanctioned the lower estimates of Rs.10,428/- recommended by Col. Napier. The alignment of the road and its level remained unchanged until 1920 whereafter extensive improvement were carried out in the section near General Post Office crossing and elsewhere. It was, later on, that the whole length of the Mall Road was remoulded on its present lines under the personal supervision of Mr. Ducane Smythe, the Chief Engineer whose work in turn was supervised directly by Lt. Governor of Punjab, Sir Charlas Rivaz. The old written accounts of Lahore indicate that it was nothing unusual to meet on wintery mornings, all the high officials in the earnest consultation by the road side and sometimes Sir Charlas Rivaz would be measuring the alignment with measuring tape in his own hands. Sir Charlas Rivaz was very particular about felling of trees on this road especially when this was being widened and re-aligned around the Mayo School of Arts. The name Mall, of the Road starting from Mayo School of arts round-about to the entry point of Mian Mir Cantonment was known as "Mall Road". According to one account the Mall Road was known as such commonly but in some drawings and maps it was shown as Lawrence Road before 1876. There was also no such road as Lower Mall which formed probably the road from Bhati Gate to Multan Road junction near about Chauburji leaving the District Courts, Government College new hostel, Civil Secretariat and Rivaz Gardens on its right side. The term Upper Mall appears to have been used during the Governorship of Sir Danald McLeod after whose name the localities around Beadon Road, Hall Road were named as Donald Town. The Mall Road ends on the Arts School round about in front of the Punjab University Institute of Chemical Technology with a diversion to the Municipal Hall, a link road to the west known as Bank Road and the other towards north-east connecting Government College. Further taking two diversions one towards District Courts and the other towards Law College Senate Hall and New Anarkali Bazar. The existing Nasir Bagh was till recently known as Gole Bagh or Company Bagh and there was no road in front of the Town Hall which was only provided to connect Mall with Lower Mall Road in front of existing P. M. G. Office. It may just be mentioned in passing that the Gole Bagh in older times was known as Band Stand Garden where Police Band played regularly twice a week and the beauty and fashion of the Civil Station gathered their to exchange gossip and listen to the music but this disappeared much before early 1920. The band used to perform in the Lawrence Gardens twice a week. The Mall Road of the late 1880s had few important buildings on its both sides coming from the direction of Mian Mir. There was nothing seen after crossing the canal except infertile land on both sides with the exception of a double-storey bungalow on the left side owned by Maharaja of Patiala. Further, on the same side of the road were Lawrence Garden and Montgomery Hall with Government House on the opposite. The plot of land on the end of Kashmir Road owned by Mr. R. Burney known as Burney Gardens and next to it came the old Punjab Club "a Hideous barrack like structure with its racket court at the back which explains why Egerton Road was known, in years gone by, "Racket Court Road". On this place later came up Nedou's hotel. There were no buildings on the opposite side where the new Masonic Lodge was built in 1916. Opposite the present Sadiq Plaza in Regal Chowk there used to be buildings of Civil and Military Gazette and some private bungalows. Dial Singh Mansion was built after demolition of the building known 'The Exchange'. The workshop of Bombay Motors agency and Ford Motor Company were also in the surroundings. The only building on the plain which was occupied by Judicial Offices was the Shrine of Shah Chirgah which was originally occupied by Deputy Commissioner, Lahore, later his Principal Assistant and then by Accountant General's Office.

M/s Richardson & Co. were predecessor of M/s E. Plomer & Co. the only chemist in Lahore. After passing Shah Chiragh there was no building on either side of the road. The areas now under General Post Office, Telephone Office, F. C. College (hostel), YMCA building were open spaces. This rambling description will enable one to conjure up a more or less accurate idea as to what the Upper Mall was like before construction of the numerous imposing buildings. It will be just relevant to place on record that the present position of the building on Mall (on its sides) starting from the point in front of PMG Office where it has been constructed on a part of the Nasir Bagh, in front of the Town Hal; passing the Corporation round-about, the Art School, Central Museum, the abandoned Tolinton Market, the Anarkali chowk, Commercial Building, Standard Chartered Bank, Sunlight Building, National Bank of Pakistan, G. P .O., State Bank, Dial Singh Mansion, Regal Cinema, Cathedral Church and School, Naqi Market and Shah Din Building one readers Faisal Chowk originally known as Charring Cross. Following the same direction from PMG Office onwards towards the left is the Punjab University Old Campus, Old Chinese Lunch Home, now Bolan Bank, Cooperative Building, YMCA, Grindlays Bank, Old building of State Bank, E. Polmer Chemists, Church, some stores and book shops, abandoned Ahmad Mansion, Ansari Store, Panorama, Indus Motors, Feroz Sons, Al-Flah, Assembly Chambers, Summit Minar and WAPDA House.

Moving up further on the left we find the Avari Hotel, Alhamra Arts Council, Governor House, Pakistan Administrative Staff College, Aitchison College, National Hotel, Jamia Masjid Aks-e-Jameel, Rangers Headquarters, Fortress Stadium crossing the railway line. On the right side starting from Faisal Chowk (Charring Cross) we find the defunct Masonic Lodge now known as 90-Shahrah-e-Quaid-e-Azam where offices of Chief Minister, Punjab have been housed. Lahore Zoo, Lawrence Gardens, Quaid-e-Azam Library in Lawrence, Montgomery Hall, located in Lawrence Gardens, Pearl Continental Hotel, GOR-I, Gymkhana Club and Police Lines until we enter Mian Mir Cantt. area.

It may not be out of place to mention that the portion of the road from Anarkali Chowk onwards was also sometimes known as Exhibition Road with reference to the Exhibition of 1864 which was held at the place later occupied by Municipal (Tolinton) Market. A tendency in the late 60s and early 70s was there to change the names of the city roads and as a result of that movement the name of the Mall Road was changed into Shahrah-e-Quaid-e-Azam.

The present Mall road has been widened, but without correct alignments. Many branch roads merge in it and it connects the city with Airport, Fortress Stadium and localities ahead of Cantt. especially Defence Housing Society. The Road which was divided by tree line and grassy streaks in the centre from Zoo onwards in east, has also provided with a concrete divider in the 90s, areas of Lord Lawrence's garden near Government House space, near State Bank,

Commercial Building, and Museum has been added to the road to make it wide enough for taking the load for which it was not originally designed, with population of the city less then two lacs when it was constructed, more parallel roads like the Mall are necessary to take on load of increase in traffic especially the heavy vehicles with population of the city over 70 lacs.

BIBLIOGRAPHY

1. Agarwal Lal Chiranjiva, Lahore-Old and New, Lahore.

2. Baqir M. Dr., Lahore.

3. Chudhary Ahmad Nazir, Lahore-Glimpses of a Glorious Heritage, Lahore-1998.

4. Chughati Abdulah Dr., Lahore in the Period of Sikhs, Lahore-1964.

5. Faletti's Hotel, Lahore-Brief History and Guide to Lahore and Amratsar, Lahore-1913.

6. Gazetter of Lahore.

7. Goulding, H. R. Colonel, Old Lahore, Lahore-1924.

8. Lal Kanyha, Tawarikh-e-Lahore, Lahore-1987.

9. Latif Muhammad Syed, History Architectural Remains and Antiquities, Lahore-1994.

10. Living in Lahore.

11. Malik Saeed, Lahore-Its Melodic Culture, Lahore-1998.

12. Nabi Ahmad, Studies in Islamic Archacology of Pakistan, Lahore-1997.

13. Nadiem H. Ihsan, Lahore-A Glorious Heritage, Lahore-1996.

14. Nevile Pran, Lahore-A Setimental Journey, New Dehli-1997.

15. Qurashi Samina, Lahore-The City Within, Singapore-1988.

16. Saeed Muhammad, Lahore-A Memoir, Lahore-1989.

17. Smyth, Carmichael G., A History of the Reigning Family of Lahore, Lahore-1961.

18. Thornton, Lahore, 1876.

19. Tufail Muhammad, Naqoosh, Lahore-1992.

20. Wankadia L. Vhispy, Lahore Souvenir, Lahore-1990.

INDEX

N

Index

Mausoleum of Data Ganj Bakhsh

Baradari Mirza Kamran

Jahangir's Tomb

Tomb of Noor Jahan

Tomb of Asif Khan

Lahore Fort (Ariel view)

The Lahore Fort

Moti Masjid, Lahore Fort

Badshahi Masjid (Front view)

Badshahi Masjid (Side view)

Chauburji

Lahore Museum

Zamzamah

Samadhi of Ranjit Singh

Wazir Khan Mosque

Shalamar Gardens

Minar-e-Pakistan

General Post Office

Punjab Assembly Chambers

Cathedral Church of the Resurrection

The Sonehri Masjid

Tomb of Qutb-ud-Din Aibak

Interior view, Wazir Khan Mosque

Jinnah Hall

Punjab University

Tolinton Market

Baradari Wazir Khan

Anarkali

The Mall Road

Alhamra

Culture Complex

Picture Wall, Lahore Fort

National College of Arts